A THEOLOGICAL INTRODUCTION

TO PAUL'S LETTERS

A Theological Introduction
TO PAUL'S LETTERS

Exploring a Threefold Theology of Paul

Yung Suk Kim

CASCADE *Books* • Eugene, Oregon

A THEOLOGICAL INTRODUCTION TO PAUL'S LETTERS
Exploring a Threefold Theology of Paul

Copyright © 2011 Yung Suk Kim. All rights reserved. Except for brief quotations in critical publications or reviews, no part of this book may be reproduced in any manner without prior written permission from the publisher. Write: Permissions, Wipf and Stock Publishers, 199 W. 8th Ave., Suite 3, Eugene, OR 97401.

Cascade Books
An Imprint of Wipf and Stock Publishers
199 W. 8th Ave., Suite 3
Eugene, OR 97401

www.wipfandstock.com

ISBN 13: 978-1-60899-793-0

Cataloging-in-Publication data:

Kim, Yung Suk

    A theological introduction to Paul's letters : exploring a threefold theology of Paul / Yung Suk Kim

    xii + 150 p. ; 23 cm. Includes bibliographical references and index.

    ISBN 13: 978-1-60899-793-0

    1. Bible. N.T. Epistles of Paul—Theology. I. Title.

BS2651 K54 2011

Manufactured in the U.S.A.

Test everything; hold fast to what is good

1 Thessalonians 5:21

Contents

Preface / ix

Acknowledgments / xi

Introduction / 1

1   Overview of Pauline Interpretation / 7

2   Toward a Threefold Theology of Paul / 15

3   A Threefold Theology of Paul: God's Righteousness, Christ's Faith, and the Believer's "Body of Christ" / 23

4   God's Righteousness (*Dikaiosyne Theou*) / 38

5   Christ's Faith (*Pistis Christou*) / 63

6   The Believer's Body of Christ (*Soma Christou*) / 83

7   "Imitators" (*Mimetai*) in 1 Cor 4:16 and 11:1: A New Reading of Threefold Embodiment / 109

8   Reading Paul Today: Convergence of Theology and Ethics / 131

Bibliography / 137

Index / 143

Preface

FIRST AS A BELIEVER of Christ, then as a student of Paul in graduate schools, and now as a teacher of Paul in a seminary, I have walked a long way in exploring the roots of Paul's theology. I find some readings of Paul's letters exegetically sound and ethically viable for our life today. But some other readings are exegetically shallow, theologically naïve, and ethically blinded. I do not mean that my reading is simply better than others, or that it is absolute or perfect. But the issue is whether we are ready to hear different voices in and outside of the text. Often times, I say to people: I am a lawyer for Paul, because he is not fairly understood or represented by later people after him. On one hand, the task is then how to distinguish Paul's own theological voice from the later epistles (Deutero-Pauline and Pastoral letters). On the other hand, the more difficult issue is how to interpret Paul's theology found in his authentic letters (the seven undisputed).

This book concerns both theoretical and practical issues of Paul's theology and his letters. Hermeneutically, I attempt to show a different way of interpreting Paul's letters and his theology with a focus on three aspects of God, Christ, and the believer. This way of reading is unconventional but is provoking to the extent that human participation is an essential part of Paul's gospel along with God's initiative (God's gospel) and Christ's faith. Without human participation Paul's gospel would be incomplete. Along with human emphasis in his theology, we will put Paul and his theology in a wide array of contexts: his Jewish tradition, Diaspora experience in the Roman Empire, and his involvement in the early Christian movement. With this larger paradigm based on three aspects of God, Christ, and the believer, we may synthesize seemingly complex issues/thoughts of Paul into a coherent whole. That is to say, Paul's theology can be informed by who God is, who Christ (Messiah) is, and who the believer is. All three of these identities are to be related with each other in Paul's gospel. In fact, any of Paul's letters can be nicely understood with this threefold aspect of Paul's theology. With this new approach to Paul's theology, I attempt to correct some misunderstandings about Paul and his theology that sacrifice God's righteousness or Christ's faith at the expense of individual justification. Paul's theology and ethics is larger than what we normally think. I hope this book may serve as a stimulus for students/scholars who want not only to reevaluate Paul's theology in critical, historical contexts but also to enliven his theology for today—in a world where uncritical, fervent faith does harm to other people.

Chapter 8, "'Imitators' (*Mimetai*) in 1 Cor 4:16 and 11:1" is also published in *Horizons in Biblical Theology* 33.2 (2011). It is reprinted here in slightly revised form with permission.

Acknowledgments

WRITING A BOOK IS a solitary yet collective work. I give special thanks to Daniel Patte at Vanderbilt University for his encouragement and critical input to my research. With honor, I dedicate this book to him. Jon Berquist, now president of the Disciples Seminary Foundation, encouraged me to begin writing on this topic. I also thank Larry Welborn at Fordham University for his scholarly insights and friendship during my academic career. He not only affirmed my work but also made excellent suggestions. We have had a variety of conversations about Paul's letters and his theology. James Harrison at Wesley Institute in Australia has supported me as a person and as a scholar. His genuine spirit and scholarship has been a great encouragement for me. I cannot leave out Neil Elliott, for his support and vigorous affirmation of my work. I give thanks to Dale Martin at Yale University for his scholarly friendship and support. I also give special thanks to my dean, John Kinney at the School of Theology of Virginia Union University, for his great understanding of my work and unwavering support of my teaching and research. I am very thankful for my colleagues at the School of Theology. In particular, Boykin Sanders and Robert Wafawanaka in my department of biblical studies have been very supportive of my work, teaching, and research. I cannot leave out thanking my students here at the School of Theology, particularly those who took my Introduction to Biblical Studies or Introduction to New Testament courses. My students in the Paul's Letters course tested my idea of the threefold aspects of Paul's theology.

Above all, nothing would have been possible without my family's support. I am forever indebted to my wife, Yong Jeong, for her dedication and love for our family. I also thank my daughters, Hye Rim, Hye Kyung, and Hye In, for their loving and patient presence in my life. I send a round of hugs and smiles to all of them.

Introduction

TRADITIONALLY, PAUL'S LETTERS HAVE been read through the eyes of the Trinity in that the believer's role is passive because he or she only accepts a ready-made individual righteousness from God through faith in Christ.[1] Here the Holy Spirit helps the believer to accept the free gift of God's grace but is not very distinguishable from the work of God. That is, the Holy Spirit is the Spirit of God (1 Cor 12:3; 1 Thess 4:8) or the Spirit of Christ (Rom 8:9), who helps the gospel of God be powerfully manifested.[2] Paul, rather, begins his letters with a threefold formula of God, Christ, and the believer (Paul included);[3] for example Rom 1:1 reads: "Paul, a servant of Jesus Christ, called to be an apostle, set apart for the gospel of God." Similarly, 1 Thess 1:1 reads: "Paul, Silvanus, and Timothy, to the church of the Thessalonians in God the Father and the Lord Jesus Christ." Moreover, in 1 Cor 1:1 it reads: "Paul is called to be an apostle of Christ Jesus by the will of God."

Furthermore, for Paul, the main problem of humanity is unfaithfulness to God; he points out that both Jews and Gentiles failed to live up

---

1. The doctrine of the Trinity was confirmed at the Council of Nicaea in 325 CE. For the role of the Holy Spirit, see Fee, *God's Empowering Presence*, 1–35. The help of the Holy Spirit is referenced here: Rom 5:5; 9:1; 14:17; 15:13, 16; 1 Cor 6:19; 7:34; 12:3; 2 Cor 13:13; 1 Thess 1:5, 6; 4:8.

2. Rom 5:5; 9:1; 14:17; 15:13, 16; 1 Thess 1:5.

3. Paul's theology will be examined through the seven undisputed letters only (Romans, 1–2 Corinthians, Galatians, Philippians, 1 Thessalonians, and Philemon). These letters written by Paul will be compared with those written after Paul (by his students or later church leaders), which include the Deutero-Pauline Letters (Colossians, Ephesians, 2 Thessalonians) and the Pastoral Letters (1–2 Timothy, Titus).

to God's righteousness on the basis of faith (Rom 1–8).[4] The problem is human made and thus should be resolved by the humans: "Or though they knew God, they did not honor him as God or give thanks to him, but they became futile in their thinking, and their senseless minds were darkened" (1:21). Paul continues: "For what can be known about God is plain to them, because God has shown it to them. Ever since the creation of the world his eternal power and divine nature, invisible though they are, have been understood and seen through the things he has made. So they are without excuse" (1:19–20).

With this kind of realization of human problems, the way of salvation for humanity, according to Paul, is to live up to God's law through the example of Christ's life and death. As we will see throughout this book, these three aspects of God, Christ, and the believer are essential and interrelated in Paul's theology; that is why we call it a threefold theology of Paul.

In Paul's letters, interestingly, this kind of a threefold theology is well expressed and condensed with the following three Greek genitive cases: "the righteousness of God" (*dikaiosyne theou* in Rom 3:21–22; 25–26), "faith of Christ" (*pistis christou* in Rom 3:22, 25; Gal 2:17), and "the body of Christ" (Rom 7:4; "you are *soma christou*" in 1 Cor 12:27). Before looking at these genitive cases, we will have to recognize the complex, often ambiguous, usage of the Greek genitive case.[5] If we are to say "the love of God" is great, then "the love of God" can mean either "God's own love" (a subjective genitive, where God is the one who loves us) or "our love for God" (an objective genitive, where God is loved by us). The difference between the subjective genitive and the objective genitive is simply too substantial, as we will see later. There is also another use of the genitive case. For example, if we say we are in a "sea of peace," it means that we are like a "peaceful sea" (an attributive genitive, because "peaceful" attributes particular character to the sea). Because of this complex usage of the Greek genitive, the aforementioned genitives used in Paul's letters are difficult to understand. Typically, "the righteousness of God," "faith of Christ," and "the body of Christ" have been read as the objective genitive in which the participation of the subjects (God, Christ, and the believer) is downplayed or absent. According to this objective genitive reading, "the

---

4. In this book "God's law" is used interchangeably with "God's righteousness," as later chapters will demonstrate. God's law is understood as the principle of God's rule characterized by love and justice.

5. For more about the Greek genitive case, see Wallace, *Greek Grammar*, 72–136.

righteousness of God" (Rom 3:21) is understood as "righteousness from God" (an objective genitive, because God is the source of an individual's righteousness).[6] What is emphasized here is not God's own righteousness (a subjective genitive). Likewise, "the faith of Christ" is also understood as the believer's "faith in Christ" (an objective genitive, because Christ is an object of faith). So the logic is that individual righteousness (which is coming from God) is given to an individual who has faith in Christ. As a result, those who have faith in Christ comprise "the body of Christ" (an objective genitive; members as a body belonging to Christ). As we see here, in the objective genitive reading of "the faith of Christ" and "the body of Christ" there is no active role of Christ other than the final atonement sacrifice for individual righteousness.[7] Likewise, there is no role of the believer other than to have faith in Christ.

By contrast, the subjective genitive reading of the above genitive cases makes a considerably large difference, because now the subject's participation is emphasized. God is the one who is righteous (so the "righteousness of God" as "God's own righteousness"; a subjective genitive, vv. 21–22). God loves humanity from his righteousness, which is never our own righteousness. As God is righteous, Christ shows his radical faith (obedience) to God's righteousness (equivalent to God's love). That is what we see in Rom 3:22: "God's righteousness through Christ's faith" (*pistis christou*). This means that God's righteousness is manifested in the world through him. Now, God's righteousness or Christ's faith is yet to be effective to the believer. It is possible by "the believer's having of Christ's faith" (the subjective genitive of *pistis christou*, Rom 3:26). More importantly, the believer's having Christ's faith (Rom 3:26) can be reimagined through the metaphor of "Christ's body" (a subjective genitive; Christ's own body) in 1 Cor 12:27. Christ's body now is connected with the believer: "You are Christ's body (Christic body)" (an attributive genitive).[8] The Christic body, reimagined through his life and death, becomes a metaphor of "living" rather than that of organism. In essence, what is achieved here is that God's righteousness is powerfully shown in the world through Christ's faith, and that it

6. See the NIV.

7. Interestingly, the NIV translates "his [God's] righteousness" in Rom 3:25 as "his justice" to support the atonement theory of satisfaction in that Jesus' death satisfies God's justice.

8. For the argument concerning the *Christic* body, see Kim, *Christ's Body in Corinth*, 65–95.

continues to be effective to the believer through the believer's participation in Christ. As we see here, the subjective genitive reading of God's righteousness, Christ's faith, and Christ's body makes more sense than the objective genitive reading.

Through a close reading of Paul's texts and contexts with a focus on these three genitive cases, we will see how Paul articulates the relationships between these three aspects (God, Christ, and the believer) in his diverse and changing ministry contexts. Paul's context involves his Jewish roots (so the background of Second Temple Judaism and his Diaspora experience), and the Hellenistic sociopolitical world under the Roman Empire. We will closely examine the imperial, political, social, cultural, and theological contexts of his time and ministry.[9] With this threefold approach to Paul's theology, we can appreciate Paul's historic, holistic ministry based on his enlightened passion for God's love and his dedication to Christ for bringing God's love to the world. Paul's language found in these three genitive cases engages those who reread Paul's texts through the lens of a threefold theology.

This kind of study may be called "critical, historical biblical theology" because we seriously consider both history and theology in Paul's texts and contexts. Paul's texts are treated as the historical and theological product that deals with all kinds of life issues, whether social or religious. From this balanced perspective we will test everything in the Pauline interpretation, as Paul says: "Test everything; hold fast to what is good" (1 Thess 5:21).[10] This kind of study will help us to not only learn to appreciate Paul's theology in a new way, but also to correct some of the biased readings

---

9. The topic of the relation between God, self, and neighbor is treated in political theology. See for example, Žižek, *Neighbor*, 1–75.

10. Crossan, *Birth of Christianity*, 41. Crossan cautions us that while we can use the power of reason as such, we also have to recognize our own projected image into the study of history. Crossan talks about two kinds of difficulty in searching for meaning in history: "The possible illusion is narcissism. You think you are seeing the past or the other when all you see is your own reflected present. . . . The impossible delusion is positivism. It imagines that you can know the past without any interference from our own personal and social situation as knower. Positivism is the delusion that we can see the water without our own face being mirrored in it." According to Edward Said, the ethos of humanism is still valid, and indeed should be expanded to the degree that all humanistic traditions are equally challenged, allowing more dynamic, rigorous conversations possible among different ethnic and religious groups. In this regard, he says: "Attacking the abuses of something is not the same thing as dismissing or entirely destroying that thing" (Said, *Humanism and Democratic Criticism*, 13; see 13–30).

of Paul. In fact, Paul's theology and his letters have been read narrowly and triumphantly focused on individual justification by faith, but at the expense of deeper, wider theological insights of Paul's ministry in history. For this task, we will need a critical imagination that engages both history and theology seriously in Paul's texts and contexts. The use of critical imagination can be explained by the following illustration. Suppose that a person wants to fly like a bird, which is a good and necessary imagination, and so jumps off from the mountaintop in an attempt to fly. That person will be killed because of his or her naïve imagination. But if a person devises a flying machine (like an airplane), then he or she can fly; this exemplifies that a critical mindset and creative imagination should work together. In our reading of Paul and his world, we will walk the tightrope of Pauline interpretation so that we will not lose both the historical and theological imports of his message. One way we can do this is to weigh every concept of Pauline vocabulary thoroughly in connection with issues in real life. For instance, "the righteousness of God" is to be understood in tight tension with life issues in Paul's time that involve personal, political, theological, and ethical aspects of life.

CHAPTER OUTLINES

In chapter 1 we will review the five readings of Pauline interpretation: forensic salvation perspective, social-scientific or sociological approach, New Perspective on Paul, apocalyptic theology perspective, and political, ideological reading. We will see the major differences among them and point out the lack of threefold theological connection between God, Christ, and the believer in these approaches. Then in chapter 2, Paul's life and his most important issues will be examined in a variety of contexts. In doing so, a solid preparation toward a threefold theology will be made. The focus here is not to write a full biography of Paul before or after his call from God, but to focus on some controversial issues such as his perception of time, Judaism, and of the law. The assumption is that if we understand these things better, we can also access Paul's thought more closely. In chapter 3, we will explore aspects of a threefold theology in 1 Corinthians, Romans, and Galatians.

Then, in chapters 4–6, we will investigate the root of Paul's theology in a much larger historical, social, political, and literary context with a focus on the three aspects of God, Christ, and the believer. In all of these contexts, the three genitive cases ("righteousness of God," "faith of Christ," and "body of Christ") will be thoroughly examined. In each of these chapters, a general order will be followed: an overview of the current scholarship related to each genitive construction, sections on Second-Temple Judaism and the Greco-Roman world, and interpretation of the genitive phrases within Paul's letters. For example, in the beginning of chapter 4 we will see how the "righteousness of God" in Pauline scholarship is understood. Then we go on to see how this phrase can be understood from various comparative perspectives: Second-Temple Judaism and Diaspora life experience, the Greco-Roman world, and Paul's gospel in particular. Lastly, incorporating all of Paul's possible background or insights gained from his historical, cultural context, we will attempt to interpret the said genitive case in Paul's letters. Likewise, chapter 5 will deal with "Christ's faith," and chapter 6 with "Christ's body." In chapters 4–6 the focus is twofold: expanding into the diverse aspects of human life through history and people, and elucidating Paul's gospel of a threefold theology based on the "subjective participation" of God, Christ, and the believer. In chapter 7, through an examination of a threefold theology, we will reread "imitation" language in 1 Cor 4:16 and 11:1. Chapter 8 concludes the book by drawing upon the convergence of Paul's theology and ethics.

1

Overview of Pauline Interpretation

Paul and his letters have been read variously. As during his lifetime, Paul is intensely disliked by some and intensely loved by others, depending on their life contexts and theological perspectives. Differences among scholars are as great as the distance between heaven and earth. Overall, Paul has been understood either fairly but partially or unfairly and poorly, in some cases with an emphasis on a certain view of life at the expense of diversity.[1] For our review, the current Pauline interpretation will be divided into the following five categories: a forensic salvation perspective, a social-scientific or sociological approach, the New Perspective on Paul, an apocalyptic theology perspective, and a political or ideological reading.[2] The breakdown of Pauline scholarship here is heuristic, and it provides us with an overall picture of the current scholarship. We will see major differences among them and compare them with each other. The goal of this chapter is, while surfacing limitedness or partiality in the various scholarly approaches to Paul and his letters, to implicate an alternative reading of Paul's theology that involves God, Christ, and the believer.

FORENSIC SALVATION PERSPECTIVE

The forensic salvation perspective focuses in Rom 3:21–26 on individual righteousness ("a righteousness from God," an objective genitive case), which comes from God through a believer's "faith in Christ" (an objective

---

1. Ehrensperger, *That We May Be Mutually Encouraged*, 177–94.
2. For an extensive treatment of various approaches to Paul, see Zetterholm, *Approaches to Paul*, 33–224.

genitive case).³ "Faith in Christ" means believers' acceptance of Christ's sacrifice once and for all. From the perspective of forensic salvation, Jesus' death is understood in any of the following ways: (1) it satisfies "God's justice" (satisfaction theory of atonement), and as a result sinners are forgiven and declared to be innocent or righteous (like a judge's verdict in the court);⁴ (2) it is the price of the ransom for sinners' release from the devil's hold (ransom theory);⁵ (3) it is substitutionary punishment on behalf of sinners (penal substitution).⁶ Though all of these options are different in their particularities, they all agree that Jesus' death has to do with an individual righteousness. This forensic reading certainly helps individual Christians to appreciate the importance of the personal salvation secured in Christ's sacrifice and the joy of belonging to God. But if the whole gospel of Paul is read only through this lens of forensic salvation, we will lose the significance of Paul's gospel in relation to the sociopolitical dimensions of life and the world.

Therefore, the major weakness of this forensic reading has to do with an individualization of God's righteousness ("a righteousness from God") and the believer's lack of participation in Christ ("faith in Christ" instead of "Christ's faith"). Because of this individualization of God's righteousness, God is treated as a mere distributer of righteousness to individuals who have faith in Christ. The scope of God's children is confined to the church only. The implication is that there are two kinds of people: people who belong to Christ and people who belong to the world (non-believers). Because of this kind of individualization of God's righteousness and a possible danger of exclusivism, what is sacrificed is not only God's "universal" righteousness that concerns all people, but also the role of God as an actor of love and righteousness, not merely a source of it or a judge in the court. At the core of this kind of reductionism is a "feel-good gospel that Jesus died instead of me; so I do not die." But if we take the theory of "moral sacrifice" on the meaning of Jesus' death, the message is very different from the previous perspective of forensic salvation: "Jesus died

---

3. See Reasoner, *Romans in Full Circle*, 23–41.

4. See Jennings Jr., *Transforming Atonement*, 13–28. See also Loewe, *Christology*, 165–66.

5. Jennings Jr., *Transforming Atonement*, 217–20. Loewe, *Christology*, 95.

6. Jennings Jr., *Transforming Atonement*, 13, 221. Loewe, *Christology*, 88.

because we did not want to die." That is, the problem is human disobedience to the law of God (equivalent to God's righteousness).[7]

In sum, despite some benefits of the forensic salvation understanding, such as secure identity in Christ, the primary weakness is that there is no participation of the subjects (God, Christ, and the believer). That is, God is a mere judge or source of righteousness, Christ Jesus is a perfect sacrifice for individual justification once and for all, and the believer receives benefits without a cost. Likewise, the problem is there is a separation between theology and ethics. Because the believer's identity is fixed and secured in Christ once and for all, ethics is only secondary, and so there is no room for self-criticism.

SOCIAL-SCIENTIFIC OR SOCIOLOGICAL APPROACH

The social-scientific or sociological approach analyzes Paul and his letters with a focus on the social aspects of Paul's communities and beyond them. Various forms of social and community life are examined through social-scientific or sociological approaches. Though these two approaches are different in terms of their different models or theories, their purpose is, more or less, the same: to understand and explain social issues such as boundary and identity of the community. The basic assumption of this social-scientific approach starts with the nature of humanity as a social being, which finds meaning in the community or in the society in which even theology is formed. While the social body metaphor, borrowed from the Stoic concord (*homonoia*) speeches,[8] aims at the unity of community, social and cultural anthropology looks at culturally constructed boundary issues.[9] Functionalist sociology relates to how the entire community or society functions for the goal of harmony and perpetual survival likely

---

7. Jennings Jr., *Transforming Atonement*, 225.

8. The social body metaphor aims at unity or concord (*homonoia*). Society as body is one, so all members should stay in agreement with each other for the greater cause of the unity of body-society. Margarett Mitchell, for example, reads 1 Corinthians as a deliberative rhetoric aimed at the unity of the community as body at the time of divisions in the community. See Mitchell, *Paul's Rhetoric of Reconciliation*, 20–64.

9. Cultural or social anthropology primarily deals with cultural aspects of human life. For example, Mary Douglas suggests that the issue of purity or dirt has to do with symbolic boundary maintenance. See Douglas, *Purity and Danger*, 114–15. With a similar concern, Jerome Neyrey reads Paul's body metaphor in terms of a bounded system that should prevent impurity or other dangers from outside of the community. See Neyrey, *Paul in Other Worlds*, 116.

in biological organism;[10] sociology of knowledge explains how a certain diffident community (members' lack of confidence in the community, for example) is maintained because of special knowledge that serves as a "symbolic universe" or "social canopy."[11] Despite all these different foci, the common ground in these social-scientific, sociological approaches is that Paul is viewed as a skillful, realistic thinker in the matters of community,[12] as a community organizer who is concerned about the purity and maintenance of it. Paul is known for adopting the conventional value or philosophy of the time, especially the ideal of Hellenistic unity (*homonoia*), around which Paul's communities are constructed.[13] Likewise, Paul becomes a revelatory power or authority—a privileged apostle because of his work and identity that were given by God.

In conclusion, all of the readings in this approach shed new light on Paul's handling of the community by focusing on the social behavior of individuals and of the community. However, the major weakness is in this approach is that it also does not look into the role of God's righteousness nor does it look into Christ's radical faith in terms of his challenge to society's norm. Faith in Christ (rather than Christ's faithfulness) becomes a sort of bonding glue that allows members to stay in the community with a comfortable sense of identity. Likewise, there is no active role of the believer. In fact, we can even read Paul's metaphor of "the body of

10. Earlier functionalism goes back to Durkheim. The idea of functionalism comes from the view of the biological organism, so society is viewed likewise. Society as a whole, like the human body, is maintained through self-defense or adjustment for the goal of harmony. Different functions of society work together to maintain the whole society. Even when a moment of crisis occurs in community, there arise some social functions to mete out this tension created by crisis. Gerd Theissen, for example, reads the Corinthians community from this perspective. That is, the wealthy, powerful benefactors in the community help maintain the Corinthian community by providing necessary means for the community. Theissen calls this kind of community "love-patriarchalism." See Theissen, *Social Setting of Pauline Christianity*, 36–37, 96–99, 121–40.

11. Sociology of knowledge, as one aspect of sociology, explains how, for instance, an isolated or unstable community is encouraged to stay in with confidence; that is, the main influence for staying in the community is because they are provided a "symbolic universe" (or social canopy) through language (knowledge) that legitimates members' choice of the community. See Berger, *Social Construction of Reality*, 92–128. See also Berger, *Sacred Canopy*, 21–40.

12. Francis Watson argues that Paul is a sectarian leader who is concerned about his own community's well-being only, moving away from the Jewish way of life and community. See Watson, *Paul, Judaism, and the Gentiles*, 25.

13. Mitchell, *Paul's Rhetoric of Reconciliation*, 20–64.

Christ" with a focus on the believer's radical Christ-like faith. If "the body of Christ" mentioned in Romans and 1 Corinthians can be reimagined as the body of Christ crucified, then this body metaphor goes beyond a metaphoric organism or "symbolic universe." In this case, the body metaphor serves as both a critique of and comfort for Paul's community. The strong in the community and/or in society are challenged by ignoring the power and wisdom of God, because the cross of Christ is the price of justice. The weak or the marginalized are comforted because the cross is a symbol of God's solidarity with them.

THE NEW PERSPECTIVE ON PAUL

The reading of the New Perspective on Paul shifts the interpretive gauge from an individual justification issue to a communal relational issue (how to become people of God).[14] In this reading Paul does not negate Judaism or the law just because it is outdated or an impossible means for human righteousness. As E. P. Sanders points out, works righteousness is not a primary paradigm for Jewish people in first-century CE Palestine. Jews also believe in the grace of God and stay in the covenantal community by keeping the law—not to earn salvation but to love God. In this reading the primary issue is not an individual one, that is, how the individual is to be saved, but a communal, relational issue, that is, how Jews and Gentiles alike become children of God, overcoming, for example, Jewish ethnocentrism on the basis of particular forms of the law. In that "the works of the law" (*erga nomou*, Gal 2:16) refer to a specific set of laws (such as circumcision or dietary laws), they set a boundary between Jews and other peoples.

This reading certainly complements the earlier readings to the extent that Paul's vision includes the compassionate God of all people. The

14. The seed of the New Perspective on Paul began with E. P. Sanders's observation that Paul's view of Judaism is not based on the so-called legalism of Judaism. Sander's position about Paul is interesting as he says: "the only problem of Judaism for Paul is it is not Christianity" (*Paul and Palestinian Judaism*, 552). Krister Stedahl presents this view of the New Perspective very well, as he centers on the issue of Jewish-Gentile relations. See Stendahl, *Paul among Jews and Gentiles*, 78–97. See also his *Final Account*, 9–20. James D. G. Dunn points out the problem of ethnocentrism of Jewish people in Paul's time, not the problem of the law per se. See Dunn, *Theology of Paul the Apostle*, 354–59. See also Wright, *What Saint Paul Really Said*, 122, 132. Though different in detail, Douglas Campbell's reading of Paul is close to the New Perspective in the sense that Jewish law is not the problem for Paul. But his reading is also close to the apocalyptic reading of Paul in a certain sense. For example, God's new time dawned radically through the Christ event (his death and resurrection) through which the powers of sin and death were destroyed.

conception of community is big enough, and the God of the Jews continues with Jesus and Paul without discontinuity from Judaism. Likewise, Christ does not terminate the law but fulfills it (Rom 10:4). Christ Jesus as the Messiah ushers in a new time, inviting the believer to participate in Christ. Here Paul is viewed primarily as a visionary and a practical missionary who follows (imitates) the God of compassion for all people, both Jews and Greeks. However, the weakness of this reading is found in that the Jewish-Gentile relation subsumes other aspects of Paul's multifaceted theology; for example, the role of personal agency and the larger cultural, political environments of Paul's time are deemphasized. There is no discussion about the role of the believer or of Christ's faith other than that faith in Christ (an objective genitive) is a condition for becoming the new people of God.[15] Christ's faith (a subjective genitive) is not discussed in social or political environments during Paul's time. Overall, there is no clear picture of Paul's theology that involves the role of God, of Christ, and of the believer.

APOCALYPTIC THEOLOGY PERSPECTIVE

The reading of an apocalyptic theology approach concerns God's ultimate victory at the consummation of time and how the problem of theodicy (God's justice) is resolved at that point.[16] So here Paul is viewed as an apocalyptic theologian who looks for the future salvation of those who stay in Christ. The apocalyptic theology perspective focuses on the matters of time and God's power. Therefore, human participation in this world is limited or not a goal itself because the ultimate meaning and completion of salvation is not through human participation but through God. An attitude in this reading is that we should "see what God is doing in the world." Typically, this reading focuses on topics such as the power of sin and death, the existence of evil, and the problem of suffering.[17]

The good part of this reading is the God-centered initiative that checks human idolatry or arrogance; everything is revealed at consummation, and the present is to be lived with an anticipation of the final judgment. But because of this kind of ultimate solution approach, there is a tendency of

15. Wright, *What Paul Really Said*, 109–17.

16. Longenecker, *Triumph of Abraham's God*, 5–23. See also Beker, *Triumph of God*, 15–111.

17. Jervis, *At the Heart of the Gospel*, 1–14. See also Gaventa, *Our Mother Saint Paul*, 118–23; 125–36.

downplaying this world. However, Paul's theology is much more complex than this apocalyptic theology; Paul requires human response to the Spirit or God in this world, as we will see in later chapters. The main weakness of the apocalyptic theology perspective is that it does not emphasize the role of human agency in making actual changes in the world. In this view, the cross nullifies the power of sin, and Paul's gospel concerns future consummation when God judges (1 Cor 15).[18] For instance, sin's power is defeated by God's invasion through Jesus' cross in the world, and a new world is created through the power of God's gospel.[19] However, the apocalyptic language here is a bit hollow because there is no specific role attached to the believer in defeating sin. Surprisingly, according to Paul, the power of sin can be defeated when the believer puts to death the deeds of human flesh (Rom 8:7). Sin's power can be undone each time by the believer's participation in Christ's death, which is a result of his or her submission to the law of God aiming at "life and peace" (Rom 8:2). Sin exercises its power to those who do not submit to the law of God (equivalent to God's righteousness). The solution is to die to the law (of sin) and to die "through Christ's body" (Rom 7:4)—which is Christ's sacrifice and costly love.

In sum, the apocalyptic reading helps us to understand that Paul's theology involves the panorama of God's salvation culminating at the consummation. The theocentric perspective of this reading corrects the human tendency of idolatry or arrogance, because all will be revealed before God. But because of this future focus, real-world experiences and issues are not well addressed. There is no role of Christ other than making a perfect sacrifice that defeats the power of sin. There is no role for believers to participate in Christ's faith other than putting their faith in him (objective genitive). Likewise, there is no role of God's righteousness for human salvation.

POLITICAL, IDEOLOGICAL READING

A political or ideological reading can hardly be considered as singular since scholarly interpretations within this approach are divergent and often conflict with each other. This reading emphasizes the role of politics or ideology in Paul's letters. On one end of the spectrum there is a liberating Paul who challenges the Empire and the social conventions of

---

18. Gaventa, *Our Mother Saint Paul*, 118–23; 125–36.
19. Ibid., 125–36.

the day (gender inequality, or power structure within the community and outside of it).[20] On the other end of the spectrum there is a conservative, hierarchical, mimic Paul who accepts the social conventions of the day.[21] Whereas the former group emphasizes the egalitarian nature of Paul's gospel (justice, equality between genders and classes), the latter group reads Paul as one of the elites in Roman society who follows the ideal of Hellenistic unity and social conventions of the day. This sheer division of interpretation occurs because there are different understandings about Paul; for example, his background, his life before and after the call of God, and his view of the world and Judaism. Thorny, debatable issues include gender relation (1 Cor 11:2–16; 14:33–36), Paul's authority (1–2 Cor), and the view of government (Rom 13:1–7). The question is which Paul is right: a liberating Paul, a controlling bigot, or something else? We will return to this topic in chapter 7 when we deal with Paul's language of imitation. Nonetheless, the political, ideological reading complements the former readings because it clearly deals with certain aspects of social, political issues not only in Paul's community but also in society in general. However, the weakness of this reading is that there is no clear articulation on three aspects of God, Christ, and the believer in terms of the subjects' participation.

SUMMARY

The five readings discussed above have merit because each has a different emphasis on life: for example, the forensic salvation approach looks at the human problem of low self-esteem; and the political, ideological approach points out the human problem of a lack of participation in society (politics). However, one particular common weakness shared by all of these readings of Paul has to do with a lack of dynamic participation of all three subjects or aspects of God, Christ, and the believer.

---

20. See Horsley, *Paul and Empire*, 10–87. Borg, *First Paul*, 93–121. Elliott, *Arrogance of Nations*, 59–85.

21. See Marchal, *Hierarchy, Unity, and Imitation*, 1–15; his *Politics of Heaven*, 1–14; Polaski, *Paul and the Discourse of Power*, 104; Castelli, *Imitating Paul*, 21–33; Fiorenza, *Power of the Word*, 82–109; Wire, *Corinthian Women Prophets*, 45–47.

2

Toward a Threefold Theology of Paul

IN WORKING TOWARD THE threefold theology of Paul, we have to understand what caused him to change his life from a former persecutor of the church to an apostle of Christ Jesus to the Gentiles. For this purpose we will focus on Paul's view of time, of the Messiah, and of Judaism. Then, we will examine some passages of Paul's texts that reveal his theological and anthropological concerns through which we can find the role of God, of Christ, and of the believer.

PAUL'S LIFE

We have to depend on the seven undisputed Pauline letters[1] to know who Paul is and what he strives for, because other texts such as Acts and the Deutero-Pauline and Pastoral Letters conflict with his own letters.[2] Based

---

1. We have to distinguish the seven undisputed Pauline letters from the Deutero-Pauline and Pastoral Letters. Because of so many differences as compared with Paul's own letters (differences in theological perspectives, vocabulary, and issues treated), it is hardly believed that Paul wrote these latter groupings of letters.

2. For example, Acts' portrayal of Paul is often tendentious in that he is viewed as an idealistic missionary, endorsed by the Jerusalem church and its apostles. Acts tells the story about Paul with the purpose that God moves the gospel beyond Jerusalem through the Holy Spirit. Paul, a persecutor of the church, became an important evangelist to bring this gospel to the world, with the unanimous agreement and support of the Jerusalem leaders. But Paul states that there is conflict between him and the Jerusalem church (Gal 2:1–21). Paul says that his apostleship is not based on human endorsement or from Jerusalem but based on God's call (Rom 1:1; Gal 1:15) or on a revelation of Christ (Gal 1:12). After his call, Paul did not immediately go up to Jerusalem but went to Arabia first.

on Paul's own letters, what we know about him is as follows.[3] Paul is a former Pharisee, a persecutor of the church, being zealous about the law and God (Phil 3:5–6; Gal 1:13–14; 1 Cor 15:9). Christ appeared to him, as he appeared to other disciples (1 Cor 15:8). He changed the course of his life, affirming and proclaiming his call from God. Paul is set apart for this gospel of God that is manifested through Christ's faith (Rom 1:1; 3:21–22). Paul is commissioned to deliver this gospel to the Gentiles.

Paul's view of God is Jewish in the sense that God is the One who made a covenant with Israel. But his view of God goes beyond the traditional concept; now the same God of the Jews extends his covenantal love to all people through Christ Jesus.[4] Paul differed from his Jewish friends who did not believe that Jesus was Messiah. The primary change he made from his former thinking is that the Jesus who was crucified is the Messiah (Christ) through whom the gospel of God is proclaimed among all nations.

With this information, we can focus on his view of time, of Christ, and of Judaism. First, Paul believes that a new time has dawned through Christ, and will be completed at the end "when he [Christ] hands over the kingdom to God the Father, after he has destroyed every ruler and every authority and power" (1 Cor 15:24). This new time has already begun and is manifested in the community: "There is no longer Jew or Greek, there is no longer slave or free, there is no longer male and female; for all of you are one in Christ Jesus" (Gal 3:28). If anybody belongs to Christ, he or she is "Abraham's offspring, heirs according to the promise" (Gal 3:29). In addition, this new time is set against the logic or ideology of the Roman Empire, which promotes an ideology of peace and security at the sacrifice of true justice and the equality of all people. This new time in Christ exposes all kinds of human ideologies, social or political, and all forms of unfaithfulness to God. In a nutshell, the goal of the new time is to let God's righteousness be manifested in the world so that people can live in peace and justice.

Second, Paul is impressed by Christ's faithfulness culminating in the cross and his obedience to the love of God for all people. Christ's faith results in his crucifixion because his faith challenges the power of the world. Christ fulfills the law of God through his whole life so that God's

---

3. Roetzel, *Paul*, 8–43.
4. Donaldson, *Paul and the Gentiles*, 93–100.

righteousness is manifested in the world. In addition, through Christ's faith people know what faith involves.

Finally, Paul never left Judaism or rejected the law; rather, he affirms it: "The law is holy" (Rom 7:12); "the law is spiritual" (Rom 7:14).[5] He asks: "Has God rejected his people? By no means!" (Rom 11:1). The only point of divergence he makes from his fellow Jews is his conviction that the crucified Jesus is Israel's long-awaited Messiah. Paul turns a new page in his life because of this realization about Jesus. He is soaked with a Christ-like life and experience: his sacrifice and love for other people. The central image and metaphor in his life and mission is Jesus' death: "May I never boast of anything except the cross of our Lord Jesus Christ, by which the world has been crucified to me, and I to the world. For neither circumcision nor uncircumcision is anything; but a new creation is everything!" (Gal 6:14–16).

Indeed, we can hardly summarize Paul's ministry and theology without talking about his view of Jesus' crucifixion. As we see in Gal 6:14–16, the basis of new life in Christ (a new creation) is possible through a mutual crucifixion of the world and Paul, which can be understood in terms of Jesus' crucifixion because of the world. That is, Jesus challenged the self-seeking glory of people in the world; in Paul's view, the world that represents such a selfish glory must be crucified. On the other hand, Jesus' crucifixion is a result of his challenging message of love and justice for the world. Jesus was crucified for the world that needs crucifixion. In Paul's view, therefore, people have to risk their lives for the world. To transform the world Paul must go through his own crucifixion in the sense that he imitates Christ's sacrifice and love for the world. Christ's crucifixion is not a past thing but continues in Paul's life. So Paul moves on to a long journey of thorns and thistles to embody the Christ-like body, as he says that "from now on, let no one make trouble for me; for I carry the marks of Jesus branded on my body" (Gal 6:16).[6] Paul's self-understanding is summed up in 1 Cor 15:9–10:

> For I am the least of the apostles, unfit to be called an apostle, because I persecuted the church of God. But by the grace of God I am what I am, and his grace toward me has not been in vain. On the contrary, I worked harder than any of them – though it was not

---

5. Stendahl, *Paul among Jews and Gentiles*, 78–97.
6. Lopez, *Apostle to the Conquered*, 137–53.

I, but the grace that is with me. Whether then it was I or they, so we proclaim and so you have come to believe.

Phil 3:7–9 also testifies how he understands himself in relation to Christ's experience:

> Yet whatever gains I had, these I have come to regard as loss because of Christ. More than that, I regard everything as loss because of the surpassing value of knowing Christ Jesus my Lord. For his sake I have suffered the loss of all things, and I regard them as rubbish, in order that I may gain Christ and be found in him, not having a righteousness of my own that comes from the law, but one that comes *through faith of Christ*, the righteousness from God based on faith. (NRSV)

THE HEART OF PAUL'S THEOLOGICAL ISSUES AND SOLUTIONS: LAW, SIN, AND LIFE

We have briefly seen Paul's life in context as well as his possible concerns regarding his view of time, of Christ, and of Judaism. In all of this, the heart of Paul's theological issues boils down to the matters of law, sin, and life, as he discusses them heavily in Romans. At a deeper level, the problem with humans is their unfaithfulness or disobedience to the "law of God" (Rom 7:25), which is the "law of the Spirit of life in Christ Jesus that sets you free from the law of sin and of death" (Rom 8:2). We clearly see here the logic between law, sin, and life. That is, the law is from God whose aim is to give life through the Spirit, but people do not want to live with that law; rather, they live by "the law of sin and of death" (Rom 7:25) that opposes God's law. In other words, all people who oppose God's law are the ones who live under the law of sin and of death. The solution is obvious but difficult to practice. That is Paul's dilemma. The solution is to return to God's law, which is to die to the law of sin through the body of Christ (Rom 7:4). To further investigate the meaning of God's law and the solution, we will interpret the following Pauline phrases: "dying to the law through the body of Christ" (Rom 7:4), "the end of the law" (Rom 10:4), and "works of the law" (Gal 2:16).

"Dying to the law through the body of Christ" (Rom 7:4)

We have to begin with the notion of the law used in Rom 7:4. This law does not refer to the Mosaic law per se because "the law is holy, and the commandment is holy and just and good" (Rom 7:12).[7] "The law" here refers to a particular practice of it that results in actually blocking God's law. This kind of practice is similar to what Paul confesses about his past. Paul's zeal for God ended up with him persecuting Christians. In view of this kind of practice of the law, what is dying to the law is "a zeal for God" that "is not enlightened" (Rom 10:2). As for Paul, the problem of his fellow Jews is that they seek "their own righteousness" without seeking God's righteousness on the basis of love for all people (Rom 10:3). But Paul, after his experience with Christ, realized that his zeal for God was misguided or unenlightened.

In this context of the law, "dying to the law through the body of Christ" (Rom 7:4) can mean: "Declare a death to the law (the law of sin) that blocks God's principle of the law of love (God's law)." "The body of Christ" in Rom 7:4 refers to Christ's own body (a subjective genitive)—the image of Christ crucified in particular.[8] While God's law aiming at peace and life is not practiced in the world, Christ showed the way to it by challenging the power of the world and making solidarity with those who suffer from it. Christ's body represents his costly life because of his commitment to God's law (as God's love or righteousness).

So ultimately, the life of "dying to the law through the body of Christ" demands dying like Christ Jesus (as symbolized in his death, in his body). A paradox in Paul's theology is that one should die in order to live for God. One should die to the law of sin and be alive to the law of God: "dead to sin and alive to God in Christ Jesus" (Rom 6:11). But what are the particular ways of living for God, dying to the law or sin? Paul gives us an idea in Rom 8. Simply, the solution is to put to death the old self filled with a mind of the flesh (Rom 8:13). What this implies is that the power of sin can be undone by the believer's dying like Christ, by submitting to God's law according to the Spirit. If we submit the flesh to God's law, there comes life in the Spirit. The central message here (Rom 8:1–13) is not something like: "Jesus died instead of me so I do not die." Rather, the point is "Christ died and I should die too." Those who walk according to the Spirit are the ones who submit their will to God's law for "life and peace" (Rom 8:2).

---

7. For detailed studies on Paul's view of the law, see Dunn, *Paul and the Mosaic Law*, 1–6.

8. See Jewett, *Romans*, 433–36.

"Christ is the end of the law" (Rom 10:4)

The Greek phrase *telos nomou* in Rom 10:4 ("Christ is *telos nomou*") means a few things: "end, goal or fulfillment of the law."[9] Most English Bibles translate *telos* as the end so as to imply the termination or inefficacy of the law for salvation because of Christ's work. But that view is not well grounded in Paul's texts as we saw before. Paul himself never rejects Judaism or the law itself. In fact, according to Paul, "the law is holy, and the commandment is holy and just and good" (Rom 7:12). Paul makes it clear that the word of God had not failed (Rom 9:6) and that God did not reject his people (Rom 11:2, 23). Paul asks: "Have they stumbled so as to fall? By no means! But through their stumbling salvation has come to the Gentiles, so as to make Israel jealous" (Rom 11:11). The problem is neither God's problem nor the law's. The only problem for Jews is that they are not enlightened enough to recognize the far stretched love of God for all people. Because of this blindness of Jews, Christ showed "the goal of the law" (*telos nomou*), which is to seek God's righteousness for all people.[10] For this goal of the law Christ lived and died. Therefore, a better translation of Rom 10:4 can be: "Christ is the goal of the law for righteousness to everyone who is faithful." We will return to this work of Christ in chapter 5.

"Works of the law" (Gal 2:16; 3:2, 5, 10; Rom 3:20, 28)

"Works of the law" (*erga nomou*) in Gal 2:16 are notoriously hard to understand as scholarly interpretations sharply diverge on this matter. The NIV translates *erga nomou* as "observing the law," which is not a direct translation because the Greek phrase simply says "the works of the law." What this means is the job of interpreters. Those who accept the NIV translation have the following understanding of the law: (1) "the Law's own inability (owing to the gripping power of sin) to produce in people a righteousness that can survive before the bar of God's judgment"[11]; (2) Jewish legalism is viewed as works righteousness.[12] But as we briefly examined the function

---

9. See Campbell, *Paul's Gospel in an Intercultural Context*, 60–67.

10. Paul's vision is to bring all people—Jews and Gentiles—to God's house, as he grapples with that issue in Rom 11. For example, he talks about a divine mystery in which Jews are now temporarily hardened and will one day be grafted back to an olive tree in God's providence.

11. Owen, "'Works of the law' in Romans and Galatians," 553–77. See also Reasoner, *Romans in Full Circle*, 31–35.

12. Accordingly, in this view, *pistis chritou* ("faith of Christ") is understood as an

of the law used in Rom 7:4 ("dying to the law"), "works of the law" does not refer to the whole law or to observance but to a specific act of the law that blocks God's love for all people. Such an act may include specific Jewish laws such as circumcision or boasting of the law (a zeal for God).[13]

What Paul points out here in Gal 2:16 ("We are justified not by the works of the law but through faith of Christ") and elsewhere is not the problem of the law itself but the problem of human arrogance or blindness to the law of God. The law as God's law should function for the benefit of people, helping to produce more of life, peace, and justice. Put differently, the law as God's law is to be practiced through faith. That is what "the law of faith" means; it is "faithful law or faith-ruled law" (an attributive genitive). Here, faith defines the law, and does not repeal it. This idea of faith *and* the law (not faith *or* the law) is consistent throughout his letters, particularly in Romans. The real problem of the law is not the law itself but a misuse of the law or a zeal for God, as Paul himself testifies to his former experience that he was preoccupied with that. As we see here, whether or not one can keep the entire law perfectly is not an important issue. Rather, the issue is how one failed to live for God's righteousness. In other words, the problem is that "the works of the law" (such as boasting or circumcision) precede "the law of faith" (Rom 3:27). Christ's faith shows how God's righteousness is brought back to the world. So one can live righteously when he or she follows "Christ's faith" (as a subjective genitive), not by "faith in Christ" (an objective genitive). Together with Christ, the believer can embody God's righteousness. Therefore Gal 2:17 can be translated like this: "One can live righteously not by the works of the law but through Christ's faith." After this, Paul confesses his own faith in Gal 2:19–20: "For through the law I died to the law, so that I might live to God. I have been crucified with Christ; and it is no longer I who live, but it is Christ who lives in me. And the life I now live in the flesh I live by faith in the Son of God, who loved me and gave himself for me." In Gal 2:19 ("for through the law I died to the law"), the first law

---

objective genitive, "faith in Christ" (the believer's faith in Christ), which makes possible an individual righteousness due to Christ's once-and-for-all sacrifice (based on satisfaction theory or penal substitution theory). "Faith in Christ" nullifies the function of the law. In this view, "Christ is the end (termination) of the law" (Rom 10:4).

13. This idea comes from the New Perspective on Paul. See Dunn, *Theology of Paul the Apostle*, 354–59; Sanders, *Paul the Law, and the Jewish People*, 46; Wright, *What Saint Paul Really Said*, 122, 132; also Bassler, *Navigating Paul*, 13–21.

may refer to God's law and the second to the misuse of, zeal for, the law. Then Gal 2:19 sounds like what Paul says in Rom 7:4 ("Dying to the law through the body of Christ"), as we saw before. Paul confesses that his new life now is possible because of his being crucified with Christ (not with resurrected Christ!), because he knows that Christ showed what the law requires: peace, life, and justice—derived from God's righteousness. When the law's requirements are not kept or achieved, Paul's view of such law is negative; that kind of law must be stopped. That is what Paul means that he died to the law through the law.

SUMMARY

In this chapter we saw what caused Paul to change the course of his life. His view of God comes from Jewish tradition but it is extended to include all people; in doing so, Paul reinterprets Jewish scriptures so that God's law or promise included all people from the beginning. Paul's view of God has changed from a Jewish ethnic God to the God of all. He realized how unenlightened he had been because of such a narrow conception of God as only caring about Jews! What he realized was his blind pietism, which blocks other people to approach the God of love and justice. Then his view of Messiah changed dramatically, and now Christ Jesus is for all people. Jesus' crucifixion is a scandal to Jews and foolishness to Greeks but it becomes God's power that deals with the world in new and different way. The message of the cross of Jesus critiques all the power and wisdom of the world, which subjugates the powerless and the weak. The message of the cross also provides God's power and solidarity to those who suffer from the worldly power of injustices. That is where a new creation becomes a reality in Christian communities.

With this change of Paul's view of God and of the Messiah, Paul points out the fundamental problem of humanity, both Jews and Gentiles, in his time, which boils down to their unwillingness to follow such a universal God that cares for all people. The problem lies in the tendency of humans who do not live according to "the law of the Spirit of life and peace in Christ Jesus" (Rom 8:2). In a similar fashion, even the Jews' failure to accept Jesus Christ as Messiah is neither the law's problem (because the law is holy) nor God's problem (because they are God's children). Moreover, it is not sin that is to blame for everything, because it can be defeated if anyone puts the deeds of flesh to death.

3

A Threefold Theology of Paul

*God's Righteousness, Christ's Faith, and
the Believer's "Body of Christ"*

IN THE PREVIOUS CHAPTER, Paul's life and some controversial Pauline texts were reexamined to see what the core of Paul's theology and his ministry involves. For that task we focused on Paul's frequent terms such as law, sin, and life. We found that the central problem Paul conceives is not of law or sin, but of unfaithfulness as compared with Christ's faithfulness. Because of this human problem, Paul believes that human participation is necessary to recovering a faithful relationship with God and neighbors, because God's righteousness and Christ's faithfulness alone are not enough, as we will see further on.

There are particular roles of God, Christ, and the believer. God's participation is found in the Greek genitive case of "the righteousness of God" (*dikaiosyne theou*, Rom 1:17; 3:21–22). Christ's participation is found in "the faith of Christ" (*pistis christou*, Rom 3:25; Gal 2:16–17). The believer's participation is found in "the body of Christ" (*soma christou*, 1 Cor 12:27; Rom 7:4). We read all of these as subjective or attributive genitives, which emphasize the subjects' participation (God, Christ, and the believer). That is, God is the one who is righteous and participates in human salvation through his love. "The righteousness of God" is God's own righteousness (a subjective genitive), not a righteousness from God (an objective genitive) or human righteousness.[1] Likewise, Christ is the one who participates in God's righteousness through his faithfulness.[2] "The faith of Christ" is Christ's faithfulness (a subjective genitive), not the believer's faith in Christ (an objective genitive). The believer is the one who participates in "Christ's faith." The participating believer is the one who lives like Christ—"you are Christic body" (1 Cor 12:27). We will return to this topic when we deal with Christ's body in chapter 6. Suffice it to say now that "the body of Christ" can be understood as a metaphor for a way of life—you are to live like Christ, because here the body of Christ can be reimagined through Christ crucified. Now the believer is to be the *Christic* body (Christ-like body), using an attributive genitive.[3] That is, the believer participates in Christ's death.[4]

In sum, these three aspects of God, Christ, and the believer are necessary and work together for human salvation. God's righteousness is compared to the sun or sunshine, which is available for all people. We can never own the sun or sunshine. To enjoy sunshine, we need to go out to the sun. Nobody can block others from having this sunshine. God's righteousness is God's steadfast love or God's law aiming at peace and life. But in reality, some people do not want to go out to the sun because their behavior would be exposed. Others block this sun (God's righteousness) with an exclusive boundary marker (a narrow conception of God or community). But Christ Jesus manifests God's righteousness through his life and death (Christ's faith). Christ breaks down boundaries that exclude the marginalized, challenges the status quo of society, and advocates God's love for all people. While shaming the wisdom and power of the world, Christ's faith also shows solidarity for those who need redemption and empowerment. Through Christ's example of life, believers can be empowered without giving up on their hope. The believer's participation in Christ is summed up with the *Christic* body: "you

---

1. Regarding God's righteousness, see Dunn, *Theology of Paul the Apostle*, 340–46. See also Hübner, *Law in Paul's Thought*, 124–37.

2. Bassler, *Navigating Paul*, 27–33.

3. Kim, *Christ's Body in Corinth*, 65–95. For "a way of life" in Paul's letters, see Gal 2:19–20 and Phil 1:21.

4. In Paul's seven undisputed letters, "the body of Christ" is not used to refer to the church (organism metaphor), as compared with the Deutero-Pauline Letters (Col 1:18, 24; 2:19; Eph 4:12; 5:23).

are Christ's body" (1 Cor 12:27). The believer should follow the footsteps of Christ for God's righteousness.

As we see here, undoubtedly, my reading of Paul is very different from the objective genitive reading of *dikaiosyne theou* or *pistis christou*. It is worth noting Douglas Campbell's ambitious publication, *The Deliverance of God: An Apocalyptic Rereading of Justification in Paul*, in which he vehemently refutes the traditional objective genitive reading of *dikaiosyne theou* or *pistis christou*. His reading of the subjective genitive in "the righteousness of God" and "faith of Christ" is similar to mine.[5] However, my reading is distinguished from him. Whereas Campbell interprets God's righteousness primarily as liberating, saving act toward humanity that delivers the creation from the powers of sin and death, I read God's righteousness to include broader political, social, ideological contexts of Paul's time. Whereas Campbell reads Christ's faith primarily as his faithful death through which God decisively acts for the deliverance of Creation, I relate Christ's faith to his life and death in various life contexts of his time: religious, political, and social. As the subtitle of his book implies ("an apocalyptic rereading of justification in Paul"), his point is that God's saving act is fulfilled through Christ's death. Now Christians have to participate in Christ so that they may live in a new apocalyptic time. It seems that his goal of deconstructing the justification theory is accomplished to the extent that the objective genitive reading in Paul's letters is very weak. But his reading does not seem successful in terms of the overall coherency of Paul's theology in light of broader spheres of Paul's time. For example, in my reading, the Christian's faith is to imitate Christ's faith—his life and death. This Christian participation is focused on the image of "the body of Christ" understood as "Christ-like body" (in the attributive genitive). Moreover, in Paul's letters the powers of evil and death were not destroyed through Jesus' death. Believers are capable of overcoming such powers by putting to death their fleshly desires and idolatry. For me, the apocalyptic reality of new life is not necessarily to be understood temporally, either in the future or in the present, but to be understood as an ongoing life experience of the now and the future without separation between the two. Through the remainder of the book, we will see whether my reading of the threefold aspects of Paul's gospel holds true. To explore manifestations of this threefold theology of Paul

---

5. See Campbell, *Deliverance of God*, 687, 702.

we will investigate three of his authentic letters: 1 Corinthians, Romans, and Galatians. In chapters 4–6, we will fully explore a threefold theology of Paul in the broad contexts of history and literature.

OVERVIEW OF A THREEFOLD THEOLOGY IN CORINTH

It is not unusual that Paul begins his letter with a threefold formula that flows from God through Christ to Paul and the believer. Paul is called as an apostle of Christ by the will of God (1 Cor 1:1). Not only Paul but also "the church of God that is in Corinth" is called and "sanctified in Christ Jesus" (1:2). Paul gives thanks to God "because of the grace of God that has been given you in Christ Jesus, for in every way you have been enriched in him" (1:4–5). "God is faithful; by him you were called into the fellowship of his Son, Jesus Christ our Lord" (1:9).

After this threefold formula, Paul reminds the Corinthians of who God is in 1:26–31:

> Consider your own call, brothers and sisters: not many of you were wise by human standards, not many were powerful, not many were of noble birth. But God chose what is foolish in the world to shame the wise; God chose what is weak in the world to shame the strong; God chose what is low and despised in the world, things that are not, to reduce to nothing things that are, so that no one might boast in the presence of God. He is the source of your life in Christ Jesus, who became for us wisdom from God, and righteousness and sanctification and redemption, in order that, as it is written, "Let the one who boasts, boast in the Lord."

As we see here, many members of the community at Corinth are from the lower classes in society: slaves, former slaves, freedmen, and foreigners. They are dependent on their benefactors to survive in society. Their bodies are sold to their masters. Often slaves are crucified when they run away or challenge the power structure of society. They are powerless, hopeless, and miserable in the urban city of Corinth. Not knowing what to do with their lives, as Laurence Wellborn suggests, some of these most marginalized in society are involved in theatrical play, a form of letting go of the internal anger or bitterness in their lives.[6] Paul's gospel begins in this social context where the lower class cries for their bodily redemption, aspiring for an alternative community of all, not based on social

---

6. Welborn, *Paul, the Fool of Christ*, 36.

convention but on the radical choice of God's love. The source of comfort and empowerment for these people comes from God's righteousness that embraces all those who are weak, foolish, and despised according to a worldly standard.

The Corinthians heard a different message of God's love that is radically different from that of society in that all have to submit to the hegemonic, unequal, hierarchical unity. The famous fable of Menenius speaks of such a dominant voice of society. The story goes like this: "Once upon a time all the limbs of a man's body became disgusted with the service they had to render to the belly. So the hands and legs rebelled against the belly, saying 'why do you not work and eat all day long?' Then the belly answered, 'if you do not want to work, that is fine; but remember if you go on strike, I the belly will starve to death, and as a result, you hands and legs will also die.'"[7] This fable emphasizes the social bond of unity, but it is a hierarchical unity that legitimates unequal relations in society. Slaves are destined to live as slaves while the powerful exercise their power and enjoy all good things. Accordingly, the Stoic philosophers advocated such a hierarchically unified universe.

But Paul's body analogy in 1 Cor 12:12–26 does not support such a Stoic view of the hierarchical social body. Rather, Paul advocates an egalitarian community of diversity in which the weak body member is equally cared for because he or she is part of God's assembly, as Paul states:

> On the contrary, the members of the body that seem to be weaker are indispensable, and those members of the body that we think less honorable we clothe with greater honor, and our less respectable members are treated with greater respect; whereas our more respectable members do not need this. But God has so arranged the body, giving the greater honor to the inferior member, that there may be no dissension within the body, but the members may have the same care for one another. If one member suffers, all suffer together with it; if one member is honored, all rejoice together with it. (1 Cor 12:12–26)

This unconditional, beloved community of God (as the church) is built on Christ's body (not in the sense of metaphorical organism)—his sacrifice and costly love that embody God's righteousness. Christ's body is the locus of life characterized with his love and sacrifice. Christ was publicly humiliated, despised, tortured, and crucified because of his faith in God.

7. Livy, *History of Rome* 2.32.8–12.

Because of his challenge to the power and wisdom of the world, Christ was crucified. But God raised Jesus from death, defeating the power of death, providing the hope of justice for all who suffer now.

However, in reality of the Corinthian community, there are many issues that divide the community. Though the Corinthians were called by God and saw the costly life of Christ, some members were still in the old habit of priding themselves or seeking self-glory.[8] Some were boastful about their new identity in Christ, claiming their wisdom in Christ (1 Cor 4:10) while not doing what God wanted them to do. For instance, some people did not honor the weak members of the community, having eaten their food before the poor members arrived at the Lord's Supper. The strong in the community boast about their knowledge about the food offered to idols (chs. 8–11). The perennial problem of divisions in the community is a very serious issue (1:12).

Because of this kind of divisive problem in the community, Paul urges that "you are to live like Christ" (12:27) right after he talked about the characteristics of God's assembly (12:12–26), which reverses the social convention of society. That is why Paul urges the Corinthians to imitate Christ's body (his life and death).[9]

In sum, God's love, Christ's faith, and the believer's participation in Christ should work together in the Corinthian church, where unity is not established once and for all but is maintained through their living of Christ's body. In a similar fashion, the Lord's Supper (ch. 11) can be a moment of unity and diversity when members participate in Christ's

---

8. Kim, *Christ's Body in Corinth*, 54–63.

9. For many scholars, the "body of Christ" (*soma christou*) in 1 Cor 12:27 has been primarily understood as an ecclesiological organism for unity. Christ serves as an exclusive boundary marker that guarantees salvation through the believer's faith in Christ (an objective genitive). Though I am not rejecting the power of unity or the need for a strong community in the Corinthian context, the real issue or question is: How is this unity achieved? Does it come through a social body metaphor? Or does it come by deconstruction of power and privileges of the powerful in the community and society? A more practical way to talk about unity is to deconstruct the concept of unity focused on ideologies or identity through the image of Christ crucified. This image challenges the strong and comforts the weak. In this view, unity is a different kind, deconstructed and reconstructed through the metaphor of Christ crucified. As Christ sacrificed for others in the real world, so members of the community are exhorted to live through this image of Christ crucified. The result of this living of Christ crucified is the Corinthian community or church (*ekklesia*).

death, determined to live like Christ in their holy sacrifice for others.[10] In this regard, Paul's vocabulary of Christ's body (along with "the body of Christ" in Eucharist) is a metaphor of living that makes possible God's assembly (church).

EXCURSUS: Church (*ekklesia*) and the "Body of Christ" (*soma christou*)

Paul does not equate the church (*ekklesia*) with the "body of Christ" (*soma christou*) in his seven undisputed letters. For example, in 1 Corinthians Paul uses *ekklesia* to refer to an institution that is being built up in the sense of an organism (14:4). Christ's body in 1 Corinthians is not placed with the church side by side, as opposed to Deutero-Pauline Letters: "The church [*ekklesia*] is his body [Christ's body], whose head is Christ" (Col 1:18, 24; 2:19; Eph 4:12; 5:23). As time is urgent and Christ is soon to return, Paul does not seem very much concerned about the church order or structure. The metaphor of Christ's body has more to do with Christ's body of the cross, as a metaphor for a way of living. If we examine the metaphor of the body of Christ in 1 Corinthians carefully, it is close to Christ's life and death, something related to a way of life, not in the sense of the organism metaphor. The church (*ekklesia*) is a gathering possible as a result of Christ's sacrifice and the believer's living in Christ. In view of conflicting issues in Corinth (ranging from sexual immorality to resurrection), the metaphor of "the body of Christ" can be closely reimagined through Christ crucified (1 Cor 1–4). This new image of Christ's body challenges those who are wise or powerful, and serves to deconstruct their understanding about unity or community. So you are to live like Christ (12:27, the case of Christic embodiment). There is no hierarchical concept in 12:27 – "You are Christ's body." It is "you" who has to live like Christ.

But in the Deutero-Pauline Letters we see that "the body of Christ" is used to refer to the church (Col 1:18, 24; 2:19; Eph 4:12; 5:23). As time goes by, more Christians gather throughout the Roman cities. Many concerns arise over administrative matters of the church (for example, questions of who can become leaders, elders or deacons) (1 Tim 3:1–13). Moreover, the church tends toward the accommodation of mainline society under the pressures coming from the Roman Empire. Accepting social hierarchy and its relevance within the church, the early church shifts to a sense of a metaphorical organism (so now "body of Christ" is a church, an institution, just like a social body), subsumed under the category of organization. It is not unusual then to find the so-called Household Rules in Col 3:8—4:1 and Eph 5:21—6:9, which concern reciprocal duties between the unequal—for example, between wives and husbands,

---

10. Keck, *Paul and His Letters*, 49–62.

between children and fathers, between slaves and masters.[11] Whereas Paul discourages marriage in general, later epistles encourage marriage and require church leaders to be married. Maintaining the church as a unified institution is an utmost concern for churches after Paul. Legitimate concerns include "belonging identity" and how to interact with society. After Paul, women are strongly discouraged in participating in the church leadership, which is against Paul's own ministry, which included women's active participation in worship, including their prophecy (1 Cor 11:5). Interestingly, a passage of degradation of women in 1 Tim 2:11–15 is similar to 1 Cor 14:34–35, but many scholars believe that the later editors (church) are responsible for 14:34–35 (the theory of interpolation, material inserted after Paul).

As a result of all this social accommodation and internal organizational matter, Paul's radical message of Christ's body reimagined through Christ crucified wanes out and gives in to conservative voices of the church.[12] Therefore, it is important to distinguish between *soma christou* (Christ's body) and *ekklesia* (church or community) in Paul's letters. If we take Paul's use of *soma christou* as referring to Christ's own body or Christ's life and death, the meaning and implication of Christ's body has to do with Paul's central conviction that Christ's body serves redemptive and corrective purposes. That is, Christ's body reminds Paul of Christ's sacrifice, solidarity with broken, vulnerable bodies, and protest against all dominant systems. As a result, *ekklesia* is possible, not in the sense of permanently fixing the community (fixing who belongs here) but in the sense of ongoing participation with Christ's body. *Ekklesia* as a gathering of Christians is not fixed once and forever but involves ongoing participation of Christ-like experience; *ekklesia* is possible because Christ embodied God's love until dying on a cross.

In sum, if *soma christou* in Paul's authentic letters is understood only in terms of an organism, we lose the great significance of Paul's theology of *soma christou* as discussed above. Furthermore, the danger is that this body metaphor can function as a boundary marker that serves to exclude outsiders or non-members of the church. It is plausible that if people choose to believe that *soma christou* is the church they may go anywhere with this ideology of the body—a divine body and divinely ordained church, the only institution for that purpose. Indeed when Paul talks about the church (*ekklesia*) in 1 Corinthians, he connects it with God, that is, "the church of God" (11:22). It is not Christ's but God's. If we understand "the body of Christ" as a way of life, we have to live it. Only then is God's church expanded.

---

11. The household code is also found in 1 Pet 2:13—3:12.

12. Borg, *The First Paul*, 93–121. See also Sanders, "Imitating Paul," 353–63; Kathy Ehrensperger, "Be Imitators of Me," 241–61.

OVERVIEW OF A THREEFOLD THEOLOGY IN ROMANS

Like the beginning of 1 Corinthians, Romans also begins with a threefold formula of God, Christ, and the believer: "Paul, a servant of Christ, called to be an apostle, set apart for the gospel of God, which he promised beforehand through his prophets in the holy scriptures, the gospel concerning his Son" (Rom 1:1-3). The gospel is God's; God is the subject of the gospel (a subjective genitive), which was promised beforehand through his prophets.[13] The gospel of God is essentially not different from God's righteousness in the sense that it aims at providing life and peace (1:16-17; 3:21-26).[14] God is the one who declared Jesus to be his Son "with power according to the spirit of holiness by resurrection from the dead" (1:4). Christ manifests the gospel of God through his faithful obedience to God unto death. Paul (as the believer) embodies a Christ-like life (as a servant or slave of Christ). Paul is set apart for the gospel of God. Paul intends to share his experience of the gospel with the Romans (1:11-12). Through his life and with others, Paul participates in bringing about "the obedience of faith among all the Gentiles" (1:5). So Paul thanks God through Jesus Christ for all saints in Rome, because their faith is proclaimed throughout the world (1:8). Paul has a passion for this gospel of God and of Christ because it transforms people and the world. It is "the power of God for salvation to everyone who has faith, to the Jew first and also to the Greek. For in it the righteousness of God is revealed through faith for faith; as it is written, 'The one who is righteous will live by faith'" (1:16-17). The "righteousness of God" is God's righteousness, and it is God who promised the gospel beforehand. This good news of God is manifested "through faith for faith" (1:17). Christ's faithfulness and the believer's faith of Christ together make this good news of God effective (3:21-26).

Actually, the need of a threefold theology is evident in the situation of Roman Christians, who faced several issues from their religious, political, and social life. One overarching issue has to do with the issue of justice or righteousness. Difficult social conditions in the Roman Empire put them to the test: whether they should stick to the principle of God's righteousness aiming at universal, equal life for all people or depend on the emperor's law that does not provide equality for all. The

---

13. Keck, *Romans*, 41-46.

14. Grieb, *Story of Romans*, 19-44; Williams, "Righteousness of God in Romans," 242-90. See also Käsemann, "Righteousness of God in Paul," 168-82.

other issue is about the concept of community. On one hand, there is Jewish ethnocentrism or exclusivism according to which Gentiles are to follow a Jewish way of life. Similarly, there is also tension between Jews and Gentile Christians, as Roman historian Suetonius records: "Since the Jews were constantly causing disturbances at the instigation of Chrestus, he [Claudius] expelled them from Rome."[15] Chrestus may be a misspelling of Christus (Christ), who represents Christian missionaries in Rome. On the other hand, there is also a problem of Gentile arrogance toward Jews and Jewish Christians, posing a great danger to the Roman Christian communities. As time goes by, Gentile Christians become more narrow-minded in their view of God, of the law, and of Judaism, being intolerant of the Jewish presence in their lives.

In view of this dire situation in Rome, it is necessary for Paul to begin his letter with "the gospel of God" that reaches all people, both Jews and Gentiles. The gospel of God pointedly addresses the problem of Jewish exclusivism and Gentile arrogance. To point out this problem of both Jews and Gentiles, Paul emphasizes God's wisdom, God's providence, and God's mercy in Rom 9–11. Nobody speaks for God as if one could know all about God or about others: "O the depth of the riches and wisdom and knowledge of God! How unsearchable are his judgments and how inscrutable his ways! 'For who has known the mind of the Lord? Or who has been his counselor?' 'Or who has given a gift to him, to receive a gift in return?' For from him and through him and to him are all things. To him be the glory for ever. Amen" (11:33–36).

But God's gospel alone is not sufficient in Paul's gospel—the threefold theology needs the three parties of God, Christ, and the believer. Thus Paul clearly states that God's gospel is about Christ (1:3), who showed the world his faithful obedience (1:16–17; 3:21–26). Since God's gospel is equivalent to God's law in ways that aims at providing both life and peace, Christ's faith fulfills the goal of the law (10:4).[16] Christ's life and death reveals the importance of God's law for all people, because all need peace, life, and justice.

---

15. Suetonius, *Lives of the Caesars*, Claudius 5.25.4.

16. As we saw in the previous chapter, in Paul's view the law is not Torah per se but refers to specific practice of the law in human community, including exclusivism, unilateralism, and a zeal for God. Often the law becomes a norm that pushes other people to conform to a certain way of life at the sacrifice of love and justice for all. Therefore Christ as goal of the law shows what people have to live for.

Yet, even Christ's faith alone is not sufficient in Paul's gospel. The believer should participate in Christ's faith since all fall short of God's glory (chs. 2–3). All, Jews and Greeks, did not seek God's righteousness. All lived with unfaithfulness. Jews, knowing God's will through the law, failed. Gentiles, knowing who God is through creation and from their heart, failed. This universal problem can be resolved only through the recovery of faith: "through faith for faith" (1:17). Here faith refers to that in Hab 2:4: "The one who is righteous shall live by faith." As we see here, faith is inseparable from life; so what matters is a faithful life that is recognizable before God. The one who lives by faith is a righteous one before God. Faith involves one's ongoing faithful life toward God and his creation. Even in the midst of injustices in the world, faithful people are not supposed to abandon their trust in God, because that is not the end of the story. Still, faithful people can engage the world and God even in a dire situation of hopelessness, because faith is the only way they can choose. So the solution is to trust in God with hopes of amending problems of injustices. Moreover, faithful persons are those who search for God's justice and peace in the world and choose to live for it even in the midst of rampaging evil in the world.

In sum, with these three aspects involved in human salvation, God's righteousness is shown through Christ's faith and further practiced through the believer because of Christ's example. In 3:21–26, the believer has to have Christ's faith (not the believer's faith *in* Christ)—a new way of life rooted in Christ's cross. This new life in Christ or the Spirit cannot happen without submitting to God's law aiming at peace and life, which requires putting the deeds of the flesh to death (8:6). Those who live according to the law of God are the ones who have the Spirit. The believer's putting to death the deed of human flesh is none other than living like Christ's body, as in 1 Cor 12:27. Nothing is guaranteed once and for all if the believer does not act out Christ's faith in the world. So Paul writes Romans to make it clear that the gospel of God is for all people through Christ's faith and the believer's living of it. Likewise, Paul also intends to share his faith with the Romans when he visits Rome in the near future, expecting their support for his mission to Spain, the end of the West.

> **EXCURSUS:** "One body in Christ" (Rom 12:5)
>
> Paul seems to be talking about a different kind of body than a metaphorical organism when he says "one body in Christ." Roman society was a hierarchical and unequal society with a patron-client system. In the Roman world, honor and shame were ascribed or acquired according to birth, wealth, or power. If we read Rom 12:1–4 through the lens of a body analogy in 1 Cor 12:14–27, we realize that Paul may talk about the human body as an analogy in Rom 12:5 as well. That is, the human body represents the daily life experience of a physical body in community and society. In Roman churches some strive for more power, which appears in the form of Gentile arrogance or Jewish zeal for the law. The real problem of the community is a lack of honoring other members in the community. How do many different members in community live together? The answer is by a diversity that honors all people, as Christ embraced all. The result of this living together through Christ's body (living Christ's death) is unity. Unity follows diversity, and it can be understood as an ongoing equilibrium. As there is no hierarchy in human body, there is no hierarchy in a Christian community. The dominant ideology of society puts the human body in terms of a hierarchical bond. But Paul's view of human body is different. So Paul says, 'individually we are members one of another.' There is no "I" without "you" and vice versa. Now "in Christ" qualifies "one body." "In Christ" can be a modal dative in the way that the believer lives like Christ, associating with Christ's life and death of honoring the marginalized and the poor.[17] In sum, Paul's use of the phrase "one body in Christ" is a metaphor for a way of living in Christ.

OVERVIEW OF A THREEFOLD THEOLOGY IN GALATIANS

In Galatians, Paul also begins with the three-aspect theology of God, Christ, and the believer. Paul emphasizes his apostleship based on a threefold frame: "Paul an apostle—sent neither by human commission nor from human authorities, but through Jesus Christ and God the Father" (1:1).[18] Likewise, Paul reiterates the sense of his call by the same threefold formula: "But when God, who had set me apart before I was born and called me through his grace, was pleased to reveal his Son to me, so that I might proclaim him among the Gentiles, I did not confer with any human being" (2:15–16). As compared with his other letters, however, Paul does

---

17. Barcley, *Christ in You*, 105–22.

18. Paul repeats several times his apostleship in the Letter to the Galatians (1:15–16; 2:1–21).

not give thanks to the Galatians because his gospel turns to a "different gospel." Paul's frustration seems unbearably high: "I am astonished that you are so quickly deserting the one who called you in the grace of Christ and are turning to a different gospel—not that there is another gospel, but there are some who are confusing you and want to pervert the gospel of Christ" (1:6–7). The different gospel is a form of Jewish Christianity that pushes Gentile Christians to follow specific Jewish customs or laws such as circumcision or dietary law. The so-called Judaizers who force Gentile Christians to follow a Jewish way of life are sent from Jerusalem, as an Antioch incident indicates. Cephas does not eat with Gentiles when people from James come to Antioch (2:11–12). This different gospel blocks God's righteousness for all in the community and beyond it. What matters in Paul's gospel preached in Galatia is God's righteousness shining upon Gentiles who therefore do not have to follow a particular kind of Jewish cultural, religious life.

Because of this situation in Galatia where God's righteousness is sacrificed or limited in the name of the law or of God, Paul preaches "the gospel of Christ" (1:7), which is comprised of Christ's faith and his death (2:16) and challenges the worldly powers and comforts the marginalized. Jesus' death challenges the wisdom of the world that blocks God's righteousness. Jesus' public execution (Gal 3:1; Phil 2:8) ironically shames the worldly powers that are responsible for his death, because he is wrongly condemned. God's power and wisdom is manifested because of Christ's bold faith. At the same time, the cross also gives hope and solidarity to those who live with broken, hopeless bodies that need redemption now. In this dire social situation, Christ's cross is a radical challenge to those who overpower others and is a radical comfort to those who need God's righteousness.

Due to Christ's faith (death) and his exemplary life, Galatians can join "the church of God" (Gal 1:3), being empowered to live for God's righteousness beyond any discrimination of people. To join this community, they should change their view of the law. They have to "die to the law through the law so that they may live to God" (2:19). Given the context of a different gospel preached in Galatia, "dying to the law" means a death to "the works of the law" or to any law that is practiced without faith (of Christ). "Through the law" in 2:19 then means a right practice of the law with faith. A person can live up to the will of God only when one discerns the purpose of the law and uplifts it with faith. What matters for the Galatians, according to Paul, is not a choice between faith and the law, or between Christ and Judaism, but a life of faith and the law.[19] Then what is wrong with the Judaizers in Galatia is their claim on the law without faith. Otherwise, a different gospel that Paul talks about may be good for Christian Jews (or Jewish Christians), and circumcision is also good for them as long as the law goes with faith. Ultimately, as Paul says, "neither circumcision nor uncircumcision is anything; but a new creation is everything!" (6:15).

To live as God's people of his righteousness, Galatians must die with Christ (2:19; 5:24). This idea of co-crucifixion with Christ means to crucify "the flesh with its passions and desires" (5:24). It also occurs between "the world and the believer": "May I never boast of anything except the cross of our Lord Jesus Christ, by which the world has been crucified to me, and I to the world" (6:14). Even the world needs to be crucified in the sense that the world should be challenged in view of God's righteousness. It is not the world alone to be crucified but "I to the world" too. It is "I" who has been "crucified with Christ" (2:19). When there is a mutual crucifixion of "the world and the believer" there will be "a new creation" (6:15) that includes all people with peace and justice.

In sum, the threefold theology of Paul at Galatia addresses a different gospel that blocks God's universal righteousness for all people. In particular, the Judaizers make disruptions by pushing Gentile Christians to be circumcised in order to be included in the people of God. By Christ's death and life, God's righteousness is manifested in the world. Christ's faith and cross informs the Galatians of the other-centered life through which the Galatians should bear one another's burden (6:2), carrying "the marks of Jesus" branded on their bodies (6:17) to continue to live up to the will of God.[20] Only then all are equal in Christ (3:28).[21]

---

19. In my view, faith and law can go side by side if rightly understood. I disagree with those who label the law as an impossible means for righteousness or salvation. For example, Alain Badiou elevates faith as revolutionary idea for human salvation, portraying the law as anti-righteousness or unfreedom. See Badiou, *Saint Paul*, 75–85. Yet, however complex it is to understand Paul's view of the law, he repeatedly says that the law is holy and good.

20. In fact, Paul's whole life (motivation, energy, direction, meaning, and worldview) is imbued with this image of Christ crucified. Simply, Paul embodies Christ's life and death in his ministry; for him, "living is Christ" (Phil 1:21–24, 3:8–14; Gal 6:17). He carries the marks of Jesus on his body, and preaches Christ crucified only (1 Cor 1:23; 2:2).

21. Gal 3:28 should not be understood as erasing cultural differences; rather, the point is the status of equality whether in community or in society.

SUMMARY

In this chapter we overviewed the aspects of a threefold theology of Paul found in Romans, 1 Corinthians, and Galatians. The three aspects of God, Christ, and the believer characterize the center of Paul's theology. God is righteous and acts toward the salvation of humanity out of his love. Humanity—both Jews and Gentiles—are hopeless not because they are merely weak in nature or born with sin, but because they are idolatrous, disobedient to the law of God (equivalent to God's love or righteousness). Through Christ's faithful obedience to God, now the believer is hopeful because he or she can participate in his death and experience God's love under any circumstance. As Christ risked his life for this, the believer is also expected to die like him. Christ's life and death challenges all forms of evil and power of the world that do not accept God's love, and at the same time provides solidarity and comfort to those who are powerless and marginalized. Through Christ's faith, the believer now sees what God's righteousness looks like and what it involves. In the next few chapters we will look into the aspects of the threefold theology of Paul in the broad contexts of history and literature.

4

God's Righteousness
(*Dikaiosyne Theou*)

IN THIS CHAPTER A more extensive picture of "the righteousness of God" will be explored in the larger historical and literary contexts of the Hebrew Bible, Second Temple Judaism, Diaspora life, the Greco-Roman world, and Paul's letters. By placing Paul's language of righteousness in the proper historical, literary context we can have a deeper or broader meaning of the righteousness of God intended by Paul. The focus of this chapter is twofold: (1) expanding into diverse aspects of human life that involve God's righteousness or justice, and (2) elucidating Paul's gospel that calls for the "subjective participation" of God's righteousness within Paul's threefold theology of God, Christ, and the believer.

"THE RIGHTEOUSNESS OF GOD" (DIKAIOSYNE THEOU) IN PAULINE STUDIES

Central to the issue of "the righteousness of God" (*dikaiosyne theou*) in Paul's letters (for example, Rom 1:17; 3:21–26) is the question of whose righteousness it refers to: God's or an individual's.[1] First, for those who read *dikaiosyne theou* as an objective genitive, it is an individual righteousness ("a righteousness from God" in the sense of imparted or imputed justification), as understood by Augustine and Luther.[2] A believing sinner

---

1. McGrath, *Iustita Dei*, 52. See Dunn, *Theology of Paul the Apostle*, 342; Onesti, "Righteousness, Righteousness of God," 835.

2. "A righteousness from God" is the translation of the NIV. Regarding the position of

is granted righteousness because of Christ's sacrifice as a price for sin. This individual righteousness also means that his or her relationship is restored with God without receiving God's wrath or judgment. In this reading, God is seen as a judge who convicts sinners and declares their innocence. God's retributive justice is emphasized along with a person's need to gain an innocent status. While Paul's texts can be read to support an individual need of salvation, we can hardly say that Paul was so much concerned about an individual justification as we discussed before. What is missing in this individual reading is distributive justice for all in the world.

Second, the perspectives of those who read "the righteousness of God" as the subjective genitive (God's righteousness) are diverse. The New Perspective scholars emphasize God's covenantal new community that includes both Jews and Gentiles.[3] In this view, God's righteousness means God's covenantal faithfulness to both Jews and Gentiles.[4] According to Krister Stendahl, Paul's primary concern is Jewish-Gentile relations: how they (Jews and Gentiles) together can become God's people beyond the traditional boundary. Traditionally, only Jews are God's people and keep the law because they need to stay in a covenantal community. But Paul extends the boundary of God's people to include the Gentiles within it.

In detail, however, scholars in this reading are not so clear on how such an ideal community is possible.[5] For instance, the issue also concerns how to understand the role of Jesus' death in this reading. For example, is the primary condition for joining this new community the believer's faith in Christ or Jesus' own faith? If the new community is possible through an individual's faith in Christ, there is no active role of Christ other than his one-time sacrifice for sinners. If Christ's faith is important in making a new community, Jesus' death can be a moment of God's radical intervention in history. Because of the importance of Christ's faith, we will fully examine and discuss it in the next chapter.

New Perspective on Paul, see Stendahl, "Introspective Conscience of the West," 199–215. According to Sanders, first-century Palestinian Judaism is not a religion of legalism ("works righteousness") but a religion of grace. Jews keep the law not to earn righteousness but to remain as God's people in response to God's covenantal grace and love. For Sanders, this is covenantal nomism.

3. Krister Stendahl points out that Paul's issue is not a personal, individual problem of guilt but an issue of the relation between Jews (traditionally God's people) and Gentiles (traditionally outside of God's people). See his "Introspective Conscience of the West."

4. Wright, *Climax of the Covenant*, 231–57.

5. Eisenbaum, *Paul Was Not a Christian*, 240–55.

Third, within the subjective genitive reading of "the righteousness of God," we can think of two more sub-readings: an apocalyptic and a political reading. The apocalyptic reading emphasizes the apocalyptic aspects of God's righteousness. The major issues are the problem of evil, suffering, and theodicy. In an unjust world where God's justice seemingly fails, the important message must be God's prevailing victory in the future. God as a final judge rewards those who live righteously. Until then, believers are to maintain their faith, fighting the power of evil. In this reading, this world is not yet free of sin or evi. Believers are to be led by the power of God. The political reading of "the righteousness of God" emphasizes the distributive justice of God. Socially, politically, religiously, members of the community must be equal and in just relations. God's justice is contrasted with that of the Roman Empire as we saw before. This reading shares much in common with the prophetic message of the Hebrew Bible.

Among all of these readings, the individual, possessive reading can hardly be Paul's view. This particular reading makes sense to those readers who need very personal help in terms of recovery of their relationship with God or who need to escape God's wrath abd gain assurance that they are justified before God. But as we saw from the other readings, such an individualistic reading may not be Paul's primary concern. Except for this individual, possessive reading, all the above readings make sense to some degree in a particular context. However, when each position takes its own reading as an absolute, we fail to see a more holistic meaning of "the righteousness of God" in a variety of historical contexts. For instance, among others, God's righteousness includes God's character (holiness or justice) and God's active covenantal faithfulness.[6]

GOD'S RIGHTEOUSNESS IN THE HEBREW BIBLE

In the Hebrew Bible God's primary characteristic is righteousness. God makes a covenant with Abraham and his descendants. In this covenantal relationship, God's righteousness means his unwavering protection and unfailing promise for his people (Ps 33:4–5; 36:5–6; 40:9–11). The Hebrew *sedeq* or *sedaqa*, whose closest translation is "righteousness," appears mostly in Psalms and Isaiah 40–66.[7] Because God is righteous, his people are expected to be faithful as God is, and have a right relationship

---

6. Price, "God's Righteousness Shall Prevail," 259–80.
7. Scullion, "Righteousness (OT)," 724–36.

with God and with neighbors as well (Isa 51:4–8). This relational concept of righteousness also has to do with *hesed*, which is variously translated as "loyalty" (Hos 4:1), "steadfast love" (Hos 2:19; 6:6; 10:12), and "love" (Mic 6:8; Hos 6:4, 6; 12:6). In sum, God's righteousness is his "loyalty or faithfulness" and "steadfast love" to his people.

God's righteousness in this case is also closely related with *mispat*, which means justice, judgment, legal rights, vindication, deliverance, custom and norm (Ps 9:8; 98:9 99:4).[8] *Mispat* is a mode of action and is strict and exact, giving each person his due. God's justice aims at creating a just community of all, as Amos challenged the oppressors who sold the righteous for silver, and the needy for a pair of sandals (Amos 2:6). Furthermore, Amos challenges the cultic festivals because it is displeasing to God when there is no justice. As Amos harshly critiques an unjust society, rituals can never be a surrogate for ethics (Amos 5:24). Justice is rooted in God's character of righteousness, which shows concern for the poor, the oppressed, the weak, and the marginalized. As people of God's covenant, Israelites need to do the same thing: "to do justice, to love kindness, and to walk humbly with their God" (Mic 6:8). Therefore, it is no wonder that righteousness and justice go side by side in Amos: "Take away from me the noise of your songs; I will not listen to the melody of your harps. But let justice roll down like waters, and righteousness like an ever-flowing stream" (5:24).[9] God's righteousness requires a life of justice for all people. The primary concern of the Hebrew Bible is not an individual justification but a communal justice and a right relationship with God. Israelites are to show their faithfulness to God as God does. Justice can be understood as an extension of God's righteousness.

In sum, in the Hebrew Bible God's righteousness can be best understood both in terms of his character and his action toward his people. In

---

8. Mafico, "Just, Justice," 1127–29.

9. It is not an accident that both righteousness and justice are needed in the society where Amos prophesies (Amos 5:24). The employed image of the stream and waters here shows the delicate differences between righteousness and justice even though both are desperately required. Righteousness is compared with the ever-flowing stream. It flows all the time like a stream without drying up or stopping. Righteousness has a comparatively quiet sound of flowing; it is like the quality of life, opening up to neighbors but with gentleness. In addition, the stream is curved and varies in shape, but flows all the way without stopping, sometimes gradually making a new way, if needed, and at other times just passing over stumbling blocks. Justice is compared with waters analogous to the raging torrent. This image reveals visible power in which water rolls down with great energy. Justice is like this; it is more audible and visible.

terms of character, among other things, God is holy and just. Because of his character as such, first of all, God is an actor who makes a covenant with Abraham and his descendants. God's righteousness is expressed in his covenantal faithfulness to Israel. Abraham did not do anything to deserve God's call. It is God's initiative, unilateral in nature. Even with all of the different images of God in Hebrew Scripture, such as father, husband, mother, king or judge, God is primarily characterized as the one who actually cares for his people in all circumstances, in good times or bad. God is always the ultimate reality that gives meaning to his people. Second, because God cares for his people, God's righteousness can also be understood as God's justice in an unjust world. The eighth-century BCE prophets such as Micah or Amos make clear that God wants justice more than burnt offerings or noisy songs in the temple. God wants his people to live in justice (distributive justice). Accordingly, God's covenanted people are to live faithfully, to be worthy of God's call. Third, God's justice also entails judgment when there is no justice in society. God can be a judge or plaintiff to defend the cause of the marginalized and the poor.

GOD'S RIGHTEOUSNESS IN SECOND TEMPLE JUDAISM AND DIASPORA EXPERIENCE

Second Temple Judaism begins with the newly built temple in Jerusalem after the Jews' return from Babylonian exile (536 BCE) and ends with the destruction of the temple by the Roman army in 70 CE.[10] This is a long period of turmoil, which actually began with the Jews' Babylonian exile (586–535 BCE) through which they realized that God's righteousness is not so naïve that they are protected from their wrongdoings or disobedience. They also realize that God's righteousness demands an ethically acceptable life, worthy of God's character. In this situation, the right response to God is a return to God.[11] In reality, new life in Jerusalem after return from exile was not very different from the Babylonian exile because they were still under the rule of the Persian Empire. Until the destruction of

---

10. Scholars call this time period from 536 BCE to 70 CE Second Temple Judaism because returning Jews rebuilt the temple in Jerusalem under Persian rule. This period marks the dramatic change of history and theology influenced by the Persian and Greco-Roman superpowers and the conflicting worldviews within Israel. See Raisanen, *Rise of Christian Beliefs*, 19–40.

11. This thought is a basis of the Deuteronomistic School, which is responsible for major books of the Hebrew Bible (from Joshua to 1–2 Kings).

the temple in 70 CE by the Roman army, turmoil was persistent. For this time period, one of the major struggling questions for Jews had to do with the existence of the innocent deaths or suffering caused by foreign powers or oppressive rulers. Accordingly, a set of questions are raised about God's righteousness: Where is God's justice (theodicy)? Why are there innocent sufferings? Why do bad things happen to good people?

In the face of these questions of theodicy, Jewish apocalyptic literature emerged in the second century BCE and dealt with issues concerning God's righteousness.[12] A typical answer to this problem of theodicy is to talk about a system of reward and punishment, as the Book of Daniel does: "Many of those who sleep in the dust of the earth shall awake, some to everlasting life, and some to shame and everlasting contempt. Those who are wise shall shine like the brightness of the sky, and those who lead many to righteousness, like the stars for ever and ever" (12:2–3). Here resurrection is a reward for innocent martyrs.[13] In a similar fashion, the Book of Revelation deals with the problem of theodicy when Christian communities in the first century CE lived through the hardship under the Roman Empire. The message is that God rewards righteous people who endure in their faith.[14]

---

12. The Babylonian exile was interpreted as a result of Israel's sin. So God's justice was not questioned, and the problem was the sin of Israelites. But the situation of the second century BCE was different because of the massive unjust suffering of Israelites caused by Antiochus IV. Pious Jews then questioned God's justice and came up with the idea of God's justice being proven in the future through resurrection. Here bodily resurrection became the means of God's justice (vindication) for the righteous. Pious Jews had the conviction that God would take care of them even beyond this earthly life because "God is omnipotent, compassionate and just." See Gillman, *Death of Death*, 86–88.

13. The seed of resurrection comes from Dan 12:1–3 during the post-exilic period when enormous suffering took place among pious Jews. God's justice was questioned. Job is a typical reflection on the problem of theodicy. Job challenges a system of reward and punishment, suggesting that the righteous people are not necessarily rewarded in this world. See Stewart, *Rabbinic Theology*, 142. As such, the theodicy problem demanded a deeper reflection on the reality of suffering. As a result, the notion of resurrection emerges in Daniel to justify God: resurrection of some to everlasting life, and some to everlasting abhorrence. Here resurrection is the means of God's justice.

14. There are plenty of evidence that God would take care of those who live righteously: "The righteous one shall arise from his sleep" (En 91:10). "The righteous one shall awaken from his sleep; he shall arise and walk in the ways of righteousness . . ." (En 92:2). "You, you fiend are making us depart from present life, but the King of the universe will resurrect us, who die for the sake of His laws, to a new eternal life" (2 Macc 7:9). "Surely, then, the creator of the universe, who shaped man's coming into being … with mercy will restore spirit and life to you . . ." (2 Macc 7:22–23). "The earth shall give up

Under this horrendous life situation where no hope is left, the hope of the future promised by God is the only comfort and empowerment for those who suffer because of faith. By the river of Babylon, Jews sing a song of salvation. By dint of Cyrus's edict, they return to Jerusalem from their exile, but their hopes are not fully realized in the face of so much opposition to the reform of Jewish life. Subjugation of Jews by the imperial powers continued in history. The long-enduring time of foreign powers as such leads to hopes of a messianic age when they will be truly liberated from oppression, with God's justice established in the world. In difficult situations where there seems to be no God at work, during times of invasion and subjugation under foreign superpowers (Babylonian, Persian, Greco-Roman), the Jews had relentless hope in a justice yet to be realized in the future.

Out of this kind of perennial hope, Jews expected a future messianic kingdom in some way. But various groups of Jews had different interpretations about this future messianic kingdom. The issue involved how to bring such a time to fruition: for example, by military means or non-violent resistance, or simply by withdrawing to the desert and waiting for God's drastic intervention in history.[15] The Maccabees did not sit and pray for God's righteousness but went to war to bring God's justice to the world. In contrast, the Qumran community took the opposite route: instead of joining in the fight against the foreign power, they withdrew to the desert and formed their own strict ascetic community, waiting for their own messiahs.[16] Notably, the Qumran community was sectarian and limited God's righteousness as effective for them only (1QS 11:2–15; 1QH 16:8–9); they are the only chosen members of God. In this the Qumran community clearly deviated from the mainline Jewish thinking that all Jews, as a collective community, will be delivered.

---

those who are asleep in it, and the dust those who dwell silently in it" (4 Ezra 7:32). "God himself will again form the bones and ashes of men, and he will raise up mortals again, as they were before. And then judgment will take place" (Sibyline Oracle IV, 180).

15. As we know from Josephus, in first-century Palestine there are different groups of Jews: Sadducees, Pharisees, Essenes, and the Fourth Philosophy. Sadducees are elites and the priestly class running the temple. They do not care for justice for all people. Pharisees are very concerned with the everyday life of Jewish people and strive to bring God's righteousness by renewing their relationship with God through keeping the law. Essenes are those who withdrew to the desert. The Fourth Philosophy is a term for those who wage war against the evil powers.

16. Räisänen, *Rise of Christian Beliefs*, 32–35.

God's Righteousness (Dikaiosyne Theou)   45

RIGHTEOUSNESS/JUSTICE UNDER THE ROMAN EMPIRE

In the Roman Empire Caesar is the one who brings security, peace, and justice to the world, through violent military conquests or through imperial propaganda.[17] Caesar is the son of a God (*divi filius*) and lord (*kyros*). Caesar is the anointed one who is destined to rule the world by the Roman deity. Virgil's epic poem *Aeneid* legitimates the idea of the divine selection of Caesar Augustus and the Roman Empire.[18] Augustus becomes the paterfamilias of the whole house of the empire. In the empire, justice comes from the power of the emperor who, establishes his control through military might or tactful propaganda of peace and security that discourages all forms of protest against Rome. Stoics supported the ideology of the Empire, advocating a hierarchical unity in which the slaves or the lower classes have to serve according to their destiny. In this milieu, human relations are driven by self-seeking competition among people. Caesar's justice is primarily punitive in character and serves as maintaining the status quo of society. Whoever goes against the empire is to be punished.

PAUL AND "GOD'S RIGHTEOUSNESS"

When Christ was revealed to him (Gal 1:16), Paul's view of the Messiah and of God radically changed.[19] His God is the same God of all, Jews and Gentiles. His view of God's righteousness extends to all. God cares for all people, both Jews and Gentiles (Rom 9:6–8, 22–24; 10:11–13; 11:25–32). His view of the Messiah is scandalous to fellow Jews because someone crucified on a tree cannot be Messiah according to Jewish tradition (Deut 21:22–23). Paul's vision rooted in God's righteousness not only extends to all people but also emphasizes God's justice in an unjust world. So his vision is unlike Caesar's violent justice and peace that serve elites in the empire.[20] Even though Paul, as a Diaspora Jew, is certainly influenced by

---

17. Elliott, *Arrogance of Nations*, 59–85. See also Borg, *The First Paul*, 93–121; Kahl, *Galatians Re-Imagined*, 21–27; Lopez, *Apostle to the Conquered*, 17–25; Elliott and Reasoner, *Documents and Images for the Study of Paul*, 119–73.

18. Virgil, *Aeneid*, book 4.

19. Before God's call, Paul was zealous about the law, and his view of God was the same as the mainline Judaism of the day (Gal 1:14). God made a covenant with Jews; Gentiles were not covenantal partners, and the only hope for them is to be like Jews (conversion).

20. Even within local provinces of the empire, the system of hierarchical power worked. Herod the Great is a puppet king who ruled Judea under the auspice of the Roman Empire.

Hellenistic philosophy, Stoicism in particular, we can hardly say that Paul accepts the Stoic vision of hierarchical unity. The purpose of Paul's universal mission is not to subjugate people under Christ or the Christian church but to collapse tradition-built human boundaries that block God's righteousness. As for Paul, Caesar's justice or peace is incomparable with God's righteousness that seeks equality and justice for all. The following table clarifies Paul's understanding of God's righteousness by comparing God's kingdom with the Roman Empire.

TABLE 1: Comparison of the Roman Empire and God's Kingdom

Roman Empire	God's Kingdom (righteousness)
Jupiter as the ultimate reality	God as the ultimate reality
Caesar as the king and the lord	Christ as the Lord and the Son of God
Hierarchical unity	Egalitarian unity and diversity
Violent victory	Non-violent justice
Blind, forced obedience	Faithful, voluntary obedience

GOD'S RIGHTEOUSNESS IN PAUL'S LETTERS

We will examine the role and concept of God's righteousness in Paul's letters by focusing on his ministry issues in context. Then, we will revisit the difficult Pauline texts Rom 1:16–17 and 3:21–26 to see how Paul articulates God's righteousness in his ministry and theology.

1 Thessalonians

Around 50 CE Paul wrote this letter to encourage the newly converted Gentile Christians and to help them to continue in their faith, hope, and love (1 Thess 1:3). Generally, the mood of this letter is warm, and the community was doing well according to Paul's wishes. But because of a newly formed Christian gathering, some concerns arose after Paul left. The biggest concern and challenge had to do with their afflictions.[21] While having joined a Christian gathering, they are still part of a larger social, economic, political network, and live under social pressures due to

---

21. Malherbe, *Letters to the Thessalonians*, 77–78.

the conflict between the Christ-like way of life and the imperial way of life (4:15–17).[22] An imperial gospel lures people so that they may participate freely in cultic meals or other activities through which they gain means of survival and security. Peace and security provided by the imperial, social network is not a small thing. Local elites or rulers cooperate with the central imperial government, dominating the economic resources in their hands.[23] But the Christ-like way of life that Paul preached means their disconnection from an imperial or pagan worship, because the God of Jews is the only true God. Their faith in one true God means a new commitment to their Christian life, changing their old habit, risking their economic life, and refocusing their life to be God-centered.[24] Thus Paul emphasizes for the Thessalonians "your faith in God" (1:8), not in Caesar or in any other lords.

Though there is no specific mention of "the righteousness of God" in 1 Thessalonians, we may certainly think of the aspects of God's righteousness in "the gospel of God" (*to euangelion tou theou*, 2:2; 2:9). First, "the gospel of God" is God's gospel (the subjective genitive), the gospel proclaimed by God.[25] In other words, God is the main subject of the gospel and the actor of love and justice for his people and toward all creation. This loving God now chooses these Thessalonians (1:4). Even though the good news of God is carried out through Christ, its initiator is God.[26] So Paul uses "God's elect" to refer to the Thessalonians (2:12; 4:7; 5:24).[27] Second, God's gospel is also about God's justice that confronts Caesar's peace and security (5:3). Good news does not come from Caesar but from God. Thessalonians, "taught by God to love one another," should "lead a life worthy of God" (2:12). They should follow "a living and true God"

22. Horsley, *Paul and Empire*, 10–87; Elliott, *Liberating Paul*, 93–180; Donfried, *Paul, Thessalonica, and Early Christianity*, 31–45.

23. Peter Oakes, "Re-Mapping the Universe," 301–22.

24. Harrison, "Paul and the Imperial Gospel at Thessaloniki," 71–96.

25. Malherbe, *Letters to the Thessalonians*, 137–38.

26. Even though the gospel is God's and many Jewish prophets proclaimed it through history (as in Rom 1:1), in Paul's view it is Christ Jesus, as the Son of God, who radically embodied God's love and justice in the world. So God's gospel is also "the gospel of Christ" (3:2) in the sense of both the subjective and objective genitives. On one hand, Jesus proclaimed God's gospel, and thus it is Christ's gospel (the subjective genitive). On the other hand, the gospel of Christ is about what Christ had done: the gospel about Christ; his life and death (the objective genitive). We will come back to the role of Christ and that of the believers in Paul's theology in the next chapters.

27. Roetzel, *Paul*, 70–73.

because God is justice. They need to change their lives and follow God's love and justice. They constitute "the churches of God" (2:14). What this implies in Paul's theology is that God is the center of the gospel and that Jesus is the Messiah (Christ) who brings this gospel to the world. Christ becomes a decisive stimulus for God's churches.[28] Third, God's gospel demands a holy life of the community. They have to make a shift in their lives from idols to "a living and true God" (1:9). The will of God is their sanctification in that they have to abstain from fornication, controlling their bodies in holiness and honor (4:3–7). This kind of sanctified life entails oppositions and persecutions from outsiders of the community (1:6; 2:2–3), but they must endure leading "a life worthy of God, who calls you into his own kingdom and glory" (2:12). Lastly, God's gospel assures the future of those who live righteously in the face of opposition and persecutions from society. At the same time, it has a consequence for those who do not live according to it (2:16). In sum, the centerpiece of God's righteousness in 1 Thessalonians is God's gospel that contains the various aspects of God's righteousness, rooted in Jewish traditions.

Galatians

Unlike other Paul's letters, Galatians omits giving thanks and quickly moves on to accusing them: "I am astonished that you are so quickly deserting the one who called you in the grace of Christ and are turning to a different gospel—not that there is another gospel, but there are some who are confusing you and want to pervert the gospel of Christ" (Gal 1:6–7). From these verses we know that the central issues in the Galatian church had to do with some people preaching a different gospel that Gentile Christians are to be circumcised in order to be Christian. Those involved in this different gospel may be Christian Jews from a local community or from the Jerusalem church. In reality, this different gospel had an appeal to Galatians, because Christ Jesus is the Son of the Jewish God who blessed Israel (2:7). But this gospel is mistaken from Paul's perspective because the good news (gospel) of God prioritizes the grace of God over against any conditions, or particular customs. Faith in God is a necessary response for this new gospel. No laws or human zeal for God can

---

28. The distinction between "the body of Christ" and *ekklesia* in Paul's letters is important. In his seven undisputed letters, Paul never equates the body of Christ with the church. In Paul's own letters, the church is God's (1 Cor 11:22). Christ is the Messiah who brings God's people to his church. See Kim, *Christ's Body in Corinth*, 65–95.

serve this gospel of God properly. The essence of God's gospel that Paul preached is God's initiative of love for all people. While the different gospel might work well with Jews because particular laws and customs are inherited to them with promise attached, it cannot properly work for the Gentile Christians because there is a tendency of cultural superiority over other non-Jews.

As we see here, the real issue is Jewish Christians' misunderstanding about the law and its purpose. Since Paul's gospel (the gospel preached by Paul) concerns the gospel of Christ (the gospel preached by Christ) to the Gentiles beyond Jewish ethnocentrism and a narrow understanding of the law (Gal 2:5), there must be no walls between Jews and Gentiles. That is why Paul harshly critiques Cephas, who acted hypocritically by leaving the place of eating with the Gentile Christians when Jewish brothers visited him. As for Paul, the problem here is not about the status of the Jewish law as such but about Cephas's hypocritical attitude in fear of his Jewish identity.

Regarding the role of God or the aspects of God's righteousness, first of all, God is the center of the gospel in the sense that Paul relates his faith to the faith of Abraham who trusted in God (3:6–9). The same God continues to call his people. Now "the gospel of Christ" (the gospel proclaimed by Christ) in 1:7 continues to witness to God's gospel that embraces all people, Jews and Gentiles, on the basis of their faith in God. But Jewish Christians pervert this gospel of Christ that aims at all people, based on their boasting identity ("Even the circumcised do not themselves obey the law, but they want you to be circumcised so that they may boast about your flesh," 6:13). Paul is clear about his call from God: "But when God, who had set me apart before I was born and called me through his grace, was pleased to reveal his Son to me, so that I might proclaim him among the Gentiles, I did not confer with any human being" (1:15–16).

Second, at the center of God's gospel lies the promise of God, which precedes the law in the sense that the latter cannot repeal the former (3:18–21). God's promise is his covenantal faithfulness to Abraham and his descendants so that they might live with God's love and justice. In this sense, Paul distinguishes between the law and the promise: "For if the inheritance comes from the law, it no longer comes from the promise; but God granted it to Abraham through the promise" (3:18). God promised Abraham that he and his descendants would be blessed through faith. This same faith is the condition of God's people. What really counts then for Abraham and now in Paul's time is "faith working through love" (5:6). The matter is not about either circumcision or uncircumcision. Through this faith "we eagerly wait for the hope of righteousness" (5:5), which means that "we can live according to God's righteousness in all aspects of it: love and justice in the present and future." This state of God's righteousness comes through faith, not from the law without faith (2:19). But in reality, some Jews were zealous about the law, being confused between the purpose of the law and the form of the law (1:13–14).[29] Whereas the former expresses God's love and justice, the latter is to be flexible in a particular life context. Circumcision can be good for Jews but should not be imposed on the Gentiles when there is a cultural dominance of Jews. In Paul's view, the traditional Jewish boundary of ethnicity or the law collapses to the extent that all people are invited and included as people of God, solely on the basis of faith in God, imitating Christ.[30] Nothing prevents anyone from receiving God's promise through faith since the essence of the law is the law of Christ, which is none other than bearing one another's burden (6:2).

Third, God's justice is to be established in Christ (3:26–28). The community of love and justice is, unlike Caesar's justice, a diversity-driven community full of honor and care, not on the basis of social status but on the basis of God's love. In maintaining such a community of God's love and justice, the cross of Christ is a central principle (2:19; 6:12–14). It is the church of God to which all people are invited to join through faith in

---

29. In Gal 3:19 Paul asks: "Why then the law?" He answers: "It was added because of [or for the sake of] transgressions" (3:20). The Greek word *charin* means "because of" or "for the sake of." But in my view "because of" is the better translation, because in the Galatian context Paul's concern is not the entire law of Moses (Torah) but a particular kind of practice of it such as circumcision or a zeal for the law. The law's function is to restrain evil and protect God's people from corruption. In other words, the law was added to make sure that God's righteousness is shown to the world. But in Galatian context, people (Jewish Christians) put this particular kind of law over faith, nullifying the promise of God that extends his love for all people, regardless of race, gender, and class (3:28). The law is not negated by Paul but fulfilled through Christ. For an extensive study of law's function, see Hübner, *Law in Paul's Thought*, 15–42.

30. The believer's faith is in God, according to Paul's theology. Christ's faith also is in God. The relation between the believer's faith and Christ's faith is not a give-and-take (cost-benefit) justification matter. Christ's faith is radical and messianic faith in the sense that God's righteousness is radically disclosed in the world. Therefore, the believer is to imitate Christ's faith. But, again, fundamentally, the believer's faith is in God. That is consistent with the view of the Hebrew Bible in general and with Paul's own theology. See Johnson, "Rom 3:21–26 and the Faith of Jesus," 77–90.

God. "The whole law is summed up in a single commandment: 'You shall love your neighbor as yourself'" (5:14).

1 Corinthians

Corinth, a major commercial port city, attracted a lot of immigrants from various parts of the Roman Empire. The majority of the Corinthians came from the lower class or were former slaves or freed slaves (1 Cor 1:26). The stated problems and conflicts in 1 Corinthians include internal divisions (1:12), sexual immorality (chs. 5–6), marriage-related matters (ch.7), food offered to idols (ch.8, 10), rights of Paul (ch.9), women's head covering (ch.10), the Lord's Supper (ch.11), misuse of spiritual gifts (chs.12–14), and denial of resurrection (ch.15).[31] As time goes by, as we see in 2 Corinthians, this Corinthian church moves away from Paul's influence or teaching, following "super-apostles" who claim they are exalted already, eloquent in speech and powerful in exercising charismatic gifts (2 Cor 11:1–14).

In terms of the role of God and the aspects of God's righteousness, the best place to begin is 1 Cor 1:26–31: "Consider your own call, brothers and sisters: not many of you were wise by human standards, not many were powerful, not many were of noble birth. But God chose what is foolish in the world to shame the wise; . . . what is weak in the world to shame the strong; . . . what is low and despised in the world. . . . He is the source of your life in Christ Jesus, who became for us wisdom from God, and righteousness and sanctification and redemption." As we see here, first, it is God who chooses these low-class people in Corinth. "God is faithful; by him you were called into the fellowship of his Son, Jesus Christ our Lord" (1:9).[32] They live on the margins of society, hardly finding any meaning to life in this hopeless world, full of self-seeking glory and other-sacrificing behavior. It is these people who hear Paul's gospel that God loves them through Christ. This news of Christ, not the news of imperial victory, is indeed the gospel (good news) for them. They find meaning in life because of God's promise of love and justice for them and the whole world. Life seems reignited for them because of their expectation of a new world in which God's righteousness and justice prevail.

---

31. Horsley, *1 Corinthians*, 51–55.

32. As for Paul, what matters in terms of his theology is God's initiative of love. In fact, he uses "church of God" instead of "church of Christ" (1 Cor 1:2; 11:16; 15:9; 2 Cor 2:1) when he refers to the church. This means that the church is always God's. Paul is thoroughly theocentric in his perspective and practice of ministry.

God wants his churches (Corinthians) to live in peace and justice by lifting up each other.[33] For this purpose, even the powerful charismatic gifts are to be used with care and control (chs. 12–14). Even the weakest members should be honored and protected, as we see in the body analogy of 12:12–26. Ideally, the Corinthian community is unlike the society where the powerful are honored at the sacrifice of the poor or the marginalized. Paul's body analogy reverses such an imperial ideology of the social body because in Paul's community the weakest members are treated the same as other members.

God also wants his community to live in fear of judgment. Both internal and external threats to the community must be dealt with so that the entire community will not decay. In addition, the Corinthians must know that there will be a final judgment before God (2 Cor 5:10). Similarly, God wants the world to know that his power and wisdom will bring justice (distributive justice) to all (1 Cor 1:18–24). The worldly wisdom and power will be condemned, and God's power confronts the imperial power that is responsible for the death of Christ. "For Jews demand signs and Greeks desire wisdom, but we proclaim Christ crucified, a stumbling-block to Jews and foolishness to Gentiles, but to those who are the called, both Jews and Greeks, Christ the power of God and the wisdom of God" (1:22–24).

God also wants his people to understand that they are assured of the future of their resurrection (ch. 15). Notice that Paul does not talk about the resurrection of the earthly body but about a "spiritual body," which is neither the earthly natural body nor the spirit. The combination of two words "body" and "spirit" is oxymoronic because in Hellenistic philosophy spirit and body cannot go together. But Paul's message is that no matter what happens to the Corinthians, God will take care of them in the now and future (1 Cor 15; 2 Cor 4). The point of the message of this spiritual body is God's initiative of love and care for his people. It is not so much about the metaphysical status of a person's resurrected body as such.

2 Corinthians

God's righteousness appears in 2 Cor 5:17–21 and 9:6–15. In the former the central message is that the Corinthians should embody God's

---

33. What is being built up is not Christ's body but members of it. In the Deutero-Pauline Letters "body of Christ" is used to refer to the church, which is being built up.

righteousness: "in Christ we might become God's righteousness" (5:21). Here "in Christ" connotes Christ's way of life, his embodiment of God's righteousness, as we see Paul's central message of Christ crucified in 1 Corinthians. Now the Corinthians become ambassadors for Christ (2 Cor 5:20) in ways that Christ performed his duties as an ambassador of God. When the Corinthians live like him ("in Christ"), they become a new creation (5:17), participating in God's righteousness by showing mercy and compassion to the world.[34]

This view of God's righteousness (God's righteousness embodied through the Corinthians) is consistent within his letters, as we see in Paul's request of the collection for the poor in Jerusalem (1 Cor 16; 2 Cor 8–9). By sharing with others, as Christ did, they can show God's righteousness to the world. Paul always carries the burden of this duty of sharing good news wherever he goes, because he knows that is the concrete demonstration of God's righteousness in the world. What Paul is concerned about is "a question of a fair balance between your present abundance and their need, so that their abundance may be for your need, in order that there may be a fair balance" (2 Cor 8:13–14). Paul's ardent wish for the collections for the saints in Jerusalem can be understood as a God-centered, apocalyptic action: bringing Gentiles to Jerusalem in the last days. That has been a long dream of Jewish prophets, and Paul follows a similar thought.

In 9:6–15 as well, we see a similar message of God's righteousness that has to do with the sharing of blessings with others. Because God provides "you with every blessing in abundance," "you may share abundantly in every good work" (9:8). The reason for this sharing is that God scatters abroad and gives to the poor; and therefore, "God's righteousness endures forever" (9:9). God's righteousness is distributive justice, and God will provide "your seed for sowing and increase the harvest of your righteousness" (9:10). The point is that God is behind your righteous work.

Romans

Even though Paul never visited Rome or founded his churches there, Romans is also a situational letter because it deals with various situational issues. First, the most serious problem for Paul may be the arrogance of Gentile Christians towards Jews or Jewish Christians, as we know from

---

34. Grieb, "So that in Him We Might Become the Righteousness of God," 58–80.

Paul's struggle with that issue found in Rom 9–11.[35] Gentile Christians think that Jews were broken off from the olive trees, and their law or place of Israel is replaced by the Gentile Christians. These Gentile Christians misunderstand that Paul left Judaism or the law altogether. But Paul rejects such claims and affirms God's irrevocable call of Israel (7:7, 14). Second, Paul also deals with Jewish Christians' boasting of the law and their zeal for God. Some Jewish Christians in Rome blame Paul for his antinomian gospel that rejects the place of Israel. But Paul again rejects such views and emphasizes the place of Israel and God's faithfulness toward his people (11:26). Third, while waiting for the ultimate recovery of God's new creation in the future, how to relate to society is also a grave issue for Roman Christians. Lastly, Paul wants to get support from Romans when he starts off with a Spanish mission later on.

In this context of the Roman situation, "the righteousness of God" can be understood as the subjective genitive (God's righteousness) because there is a particular role of God.[36] God's role is most clear in the "the gospel of God" (1:1) as it is also understood as the subjective genitive: God's gospel—the gospel promised by God through his prophets in the holy scriptures (1:2). For this gospel of God, Paul is set apart and becomes "a servant of Jesus Christ" (1:1). Now this gospel concerns "his Son, who was descended from David according to the flesh and was declared to be the Son of God with power according to the spirit of holiness by resurrection from the dead" (1:3–4). Furthermore, this gospel of God is "the power of God for salvation to everyone who has faith, to the Jew first and also to the Greek" (1:16). "In it (the gospel) God's righteousness is revealed through faith for faith" (1:17).

With this view of God's gospel in mind, first of all, the aspect of God's righteousness can be understood in terms of God's call of both Jews and Gentiles equally on the basis of faith. Paul's view of God's righteousness goes beyond a covenantal framework of Jews only. This view of God is scandalous to Jews because God is their God only, who made a covenant with Abraham. Paul's view of one God for both Jews and Gentiles is very different from the Greek or Roman concept of the highest god (like Jupiter or Zeus) who legitimates the unequal, unjust system of power in society.

---

35. Cosgrove, *Elusive Israel*, 1–90.
36. "The righteousness of God" appears in Rom 1:17; 3:5, 21, 22, 25–26; and 10:3.

Second, the aspect of God's righteousness in Romans also has to do with justice in the community and society. The weak and the strong should lift up each other, as Paul says: "The kingdom of God is not food and drink but righteousness and peace and joy in the Holy Spirit" (14:17). Making peace and working for mutual edification are an important task in communal life (14:19). This kind of community should bless those who persecute them (12:14). The instruction to "bless and do not curse them" (12:15) is hard to keep. Furthermore, they are also asked to "live in harmony with one another" without being haughty, associating with the lowly, rejoicing with those who rejoice, and weeping with those who weep (12:15–16). Avenging is not their job. Rather, Paul goes one step further, resembling Jesus' radical ethical teaching: "If your enemies are hungry, feed them; if they are thirsty, give them to drink it; . . . Do not be overcome by evil, but overcome evil with good" (12:20–21). Paul, like Jesus, summarizes the law with a focus on the love of neighbor: "love your neighbor as yourself" (14:9). "Love does no wrong to a neighbor; therefore, love is the fulfilling of the law" (14:10). As seen here, Paul's vision of the beloved community contrasts that of the Roman Empire. God's kingdom has counter-world ethics, based on loving enemies and not taking revenge; it seeks non-violent peace and justice.

Third, the aspect of God's righteousness also has to do with a new creation that will recover the original status of God's kingdom: "For the creation waits with eager longing for the revealing of the children of God; . . . the whole creation has been groaning in labor pains until now; . . . we wait for adoption, the redemption of our bodies" (8:19–23). "The sufferings of this present time" under the Roman Empire is not the last word for Christians. This aspect of God's righteousness is much like the thought of Jewish apocalyptic vision where God's ultimate victory is foreseen as comfort and reward for those going through the difficult time. The message here is the affirmation of God's love and justice: "If God is for us, who is against us?" (8:31). "Who will separate us from the love of Christ? Will hardship, or distress, or persecution, or famine, or nakedness, or peril, or sword?" (8:35). In sum, Romans is an excellent example that God's righteousness is most eloquently explained theologically and contextually in view of the Romans' situation.

Philippians and Philemon

Philippians, one of Paul's prison letters, conveys a warm atmosphere of his relationship with the Philippians. Paul received support from this church when in prison. But like any other community, this community also has some issues. As we see "your opponents" (1:27) and "dogs" (3:2), the main problem comes from Jewish Christians who impose Jewish laws and customs to the Gentile Christians. Paul's advice is basically the same as that of Galatians. In terms of the role of God, first of all, it is God's grace (1:7) that makes possible the sharing of good news to Philippians. Second, God is not remotely watching over his people but is "at work in you, enabling you both to will and to work for his good pleasure" (2:13). God wants his people to be holy, pure, and blameless, and to produce "the harvest of righteousness that comes through Jesus Christ for the glory and praise of God" (1:9–10). Third, God is the God of peace (4:7, 9). "The peace of God, surpasses all understanding, will guard your hearts and your minds in Christ Jesus" (4:7).

In Philemon, Paul writes a letter to Philemon, his Christian brother, to ask him to accept Onesimus as a beloved brother, not as a slave. Paul approaches his friend with a spirit of voluntarism, not out of coercion (1:14). Paul's approach represents the character of God who wants his people to act for good with a voluntary spirit. Paul acts as a father to Onesimus, as God is to Paul. Paul asks his friend Philemon to treat Onesimus "no longer as a slave but as more than a slave, a beloved brother" (1:16).

EXCURSUS: Righteousness in the Deutero-Pauline and Pastoral Letters

Paul's view of God's righteousness in seven undisputed letters is different from that of the later Deutero-Pauline and Pastoral Letters. Many scholars believe that Paul did not write these later epistles because of theological differences or different writing styles between them.[37] The benefit of distinguishing Paul's undisputed letters from these later epistles is to elucidate Paul's own theology without glossing over the undisputed letters.

In the Deutero-Pauline Letters, righteousness applies to the believers in the sense that they inherit salvation and eternal life once and for all. God sent Christ according to his knowledge and wisdom; Christ made sacrifices once

---

37. See Ehrman, *Introduction to the New Testament*, 291–323; Borg, *The First Paul*, 93–121.

and for all to cleanse sins (for forgiveness of sins) (Eph 5:2; Col 1:14, 20). The believer's salvation is done because of Christ's sacrifice and God's plan. Interestingly, the word "gospel" is never used with God; rather, it is "the gospel of your salvation" (Eph 1:13). The gospel is the object that a person hears. God chose the elect before the foundation of the world (Eph 1:4–5). Even the mystery of God's will (knowledge of God's will) has been revealed through Christ to the believers already (Eph 1:9; Col 1:9–10, 25–26; 2:2); the believers now received salvation as inheritance (Eph 1:11, 18; Col 1:12). Overall, in these letters God is seen as less active than in undisputed letters.

Furthermore, God is seen as a warrior in these letters: "Put on the whole armor of God" (Eph 6:11, 13). This-world events are understood as involving the cosmic powers along with "the spiritual forces of evil in the heavenly places" (Eph 6:12). Even the image of peacemaking is very different from Paul's undisputed letters, in which peacemaking is possible because of God's character (non-violent justice) and Christ's faith. Peacemaking in Eph 2:15 is possible through a way of "unity" that defies diversity (Eph 2:15). Similarly, God is seen through the lens of hierarchy. God "made Christ the head over all things for the church, which is his body, the fullness of him who fills all in all" (Eph 1:22–23; Col 1:18).

In the Pastoral Letters as well, righteousness is primarily understood as individual salvation (2 Tim 4:8). God is seen as a remote father who sent Christ to save sinners (1 Tim 1:15). Eternal life is obtained once and for all (1 Tim 1:16). Otherwise, there is no specific role or mention of God. The concept of the gospel mentioned in 2 Tim 1:8–11 and 2:8 does not relate to God's gospel. The gospel is understood as Jesus' cross only for the forgiveness of sins. Otherwise, there is no sense of Christ's gospel either.

TABLE 2: Comparison of Paul's Undisputed Letters and the Deutero-Pauline and Pastoral Letters

	Paul's Seven Undisputed Letters	Deutero-Pauline and Pastoral Letters
Major contexts	Persecution & Christian identity (1 Thess) Disembodiment of Christ's body (1–2 Cor) Distortion of Paul's gospel (Gal) Universal failure of the heart (Rom) Jewish boasting about the law (Phil) Onesimus' identity in Christ (Phlm)	Social accommodation (1–2 Tim) Disunity of the church (Eph, Col) False teaching (1–2 Tim) Lack of knowledge (1–2 Tim) Law as an obstacle (Eph) True identity in Christ (1–2 Tim)

	Paul's Seven Undisputed Letters	Deutero-Pauline and Pastoral Letters
God's role	Active participation through love and justice (God's promise, God's gospel)	Passive observer, decision-maker (Christ-sender by his will)
Righteousness	As God's righteousness Participatory (2 Cor 5:21) Manifested through Christ's faith	As the believer's righteousness As an inheritance Possessive by the believer's faith

"The righteousness of God" in Rom 1:16–17 and 3:21–26

So far we have examined both historical and literary contexts of God's righteousness. Now we will look into "the righteousness of God" in Rom 1:16–17 and 3:21–26. These passages are difficult to interpret but are theologically very important; therefore, we have to spend more time on them. As many scholars readily point out, Rom 1:16–17 contains the theme of Romans: "The righteousness of God is revealed from faith to faith."[38] The same phrase "the righteousness of God" in 3:21–26 is also hard to understand but is similarly very important.

Rom 1:16–17

> For I am not ashamed of the gospel; it is the power of God for salvation to everyone who has faith, to the Jew first and also to the Greek. For in it *the righteousness of God* is revealed through faith for faith; as it is written, "The one who is righteous will live by faith."

The gospel of God is the power of God for salvation to everyone who has faith *in God* (1:16).[39] Now in this gospel of God (as the gospel promised and proclaimed by God) the righteousness of God (God's righteousness) is revealed "through faith for faith." The puzzling task is what this phrase of "through faith for faith" means. In view of God's initiative of love and

---

38. Johnson, "Rom 3:21–26 and the Faith of Jesus," 77–90. See also Hays, "*Pistis* and Pauline Christology," 53; Williams, "Again *Pistis Christou*," 431–47; Käsemann, *Romans*, 21–32.

39. Johnson, "Rom 3:21–26 and the Faith of Jesus," 77–90.

justice for all people, as Paul begins Romans with the very phrase of "God's gospel," the first "faith" in the phrase refers to God's faithfulness through which God's love and justice are known to the world. The second "faith" refers to believer's faith in the sense that God's righteousness is to be experienced by the people who accept God's promise. God's righteousness comes through faith even long before Christ, as Paul talks about promise even before the law comes (4:13–25). Through faith Abraham believed God's promise and participated in the history of salvation. Abraham is the prototype of faith and action toward God's righteousness. God's righteousness cannot be shown other than through faith because it involves trusting, costly commitment to the character and action of God. The logic goes like this: God first shows his faithfulness toward humanity and then humans can respond to his faithfulness by the same faith. Then Paul emphasizes the ongoing, dynamic nature of the believer's faith that is rooted in God's faithfulness: "The one who is righteous will live by faith" (Hab 2:4). In this quote the righteous person is the faithful person. Living by faith is a condition for the righteous life.

But both Jews and Gentiles failed to live a faithful life. This universal failure is stated in 1:18–3:20. The point of this section is rather simple: all failed to live by faith toward God's righteousness: "All who have sinned apart from the law will also perish apart from the law, and all who have sinned under the law will be judged by the law" (2:12). Interestingly and importantly, those who are righteous are "not the hearers of the law who are righteous in God's sight, but the doers of the law who will be justified" (2:13). What this means is that faith and practice is not two different things. Even Gentiles "who do not possess the law" cannot make excuses because "what the law requires is written on their hearts, to which their own conscience also bears witness" (2:14–15). Again, what this means is that the problem is not the problem of law itself. Rather, their hearts tell everything since they know who God is and what the true law requires.

In sum, the problem is a matter of the heart—that people are unwilling to follow God's faithfulness that is shown in his righteousness. The issue is not works righteousness (legalism) of Jews but a failure of heart that does not produce good work through faithful obedience to God (1:7). That is why Paul later mentions that they were unenlightened by forgetting the purpose of God's universal salvation for all people. Gentiles also cannot excuse their failure that they did not follow their conscience that reflects the heart of God. After pointing out the importance of God's righteousness (or faithfulness) and human failure to live according to his faithfulness (1:16—3:20), Paul further discusses about God's righteousness and its importance in light of Christ's faith (3:21—26). In this section the role of Christ's faith is explained and highlighted in connection with God's righteousness. Along the way, the believer's faith is also highlighted. We will return to the aspect of faith (both Christ's and the believer's) in the next two chapters.

Rom 3:21—26

> But now, apart from law, *the righteousness of God* has been disclosed, and is attested by the law and the prophets, *the righteousness of God* through *faith of Jesus Christ* for all who believe. For there is no distinction, since all have sinned and fall short of the glory of God; they are now justified by his grace as a gift, through the redemption that is in Christ Jesus, whom God put forward as a sacrifice of atonement by his blood, effective through faith. He did this to show *his righteousness*, because in his divine forbearance he had passed over the sins previously committed; it was to prove at the present time that he himself is righteous and that he justifies the one who has *faith of Jesus*.

"But now, apart from law" makes a radical shift in suggesting a solution to the universal failure of human heart through Christ's faith.[40] "But now" emphasizes a moment of God's radical intervention in the salvation history through Christ, his Son, because formerly all people blocked God's righteousness. "The righteousness of God" as God's righteousness was shown to the Jews, being attested by the law and the prophets (1:2). In 3:22, God's righteousness is further explained through Christ's faith (*pistis christou* as the subjective genitive).[41] God's righteousness becomes a new reality in history because of Christ's faithful obedience. Christ's death is *hilasterion* ("mercy seat"); God is present with his Son on the cross and affirms his faith, as the imagery of a mercy seat comes from the Day of Atonement (*Yom Kippur*, Exod 25:10-22; 37:1-9).[42] Because of his Son's faith, God dealt with all former sins (3:25). That is God's righteousness. Now God opens a new time and wants people to join in his Son's faith.

---

40. "Apart from law" can be understood as a particular way of God's revelation manifested through Christ's faith. Here law does not refer to the Mosaic Law.

41. Keck, *Romans*, 101-17. See also Stowers, *Rereading of Romans*, 194-226.

42. Becker, *Paul*, 399-411.

God "justifies the one who has Jesus' faith" (3:26). In the following we will see the summary of exegetical insights gained from the above study of 1:16–17 and 3:21–26.

God's Righteousness as God's Gospel

The gospel of God is God's gospel, "which he promised beforehand through his prophets in the holy scriptures" (Rom 1:2). What God promised to Abraham and his descendants is his grace, love, and justice. God's covenant with Abraham shows exactly this character and act of God. The point of promise is no matter what happens to this people God will be with them. So God gave the law to them so that they might live in justice and peace. When there was no peace and justice in the world, God sent the prophets for their repentance. When there was innocent suffering, God comforts them and promises assurance in the future. Now this gospel of God is extended to all people, Jews and Gentiles, disclosed through Christ's faith, and becomes a new reality for the believer who has faith of Jesus. Because of the scope and nature of God's gospel, it includes all aspects of our lives: personal, communal, social, political, and apocalyptic. God's gospel permeates all.

God's Righteousness as God's Decisive Intervention in History

It is Paul's understanding that God marked off history by Christ's life and death and dealt with the past, showing his goodness (righteousness) by overlooking the sins previously committed. A new time has dawned because of God's decision on the basis of Christ's faith. In this new time, Jews and Gentiles need to live faithfully according to God's righteousness. In Rome there were many Jewish and Gentile Christians, and there were rivalry or conflicts between them. Jews often had a zeal for the law, forcing Gentiles to follow a Jewish way of life. On the other hand, Gentile Christians were arrogant toward Jews by ignoring their place in salvation history. Paul painstakingly warns Gentile Christians that "all Israel will be saved" (Rom 11:26). It is God's wisdom and knowledge that decide on his people, not vice versa. God also wants people to live with justice in the community and society. Love fulfills the law. Love your neighbor. Do not repay anyone evil for evil. The weak and the strong have to work together. All this is contrasted with the imperial ideology in which the powerful rule the powerless. The Roman Empire's justice or peace is maintained through violent victory or containing tactic.[43]

SUMMARY

For Paul, God is the beginning and source of life in Christ. Paul's gospel is first of all God's gospel concerning his Son. God chose the weak and the despised in the world and wants his people to live with love and justice in the world. God's righteousness extends to all people beyond the traditional Jewish boundary. It is God's justice that challenges Rome's justice. Christ Jesus is the one who showed who God is and what God wants. We will turn to the next chapter for discussion about Christ's faithfulness (*pistis christou*).

---

43. Elliott, *Arrogance of Nations*, 59–85.

5

Christ's Faith (*Pistis Christou*)

IN THE PREVIOUS CHAPTER we examined various aspects of God's righteousness in the Hebrew Bible, in the Second Temple Period, and in Paul's letters. God's righteousness is a main theme of both the Hebrew Bible and Paul's letters. But Paul extends the scope and content of God's righteousness to include both Jews and Gentiles. God's righteousness was testified through the law and the prophets and manifested through Christ's faith that culminated in his death.[1] That is where we begin this chapter. This chapter will proceed with steps similar to those in the previous chapter. First, we will sketch the current scholarship about the genitive case *pistis christou*. Then we will investigate the role of Christ (Messiah) ("the anointed one") in the Hebrew Bible, the Second Temple Period, and the Greco-Roman world. After this, we will examine the role of Christ and *pistis christou* in Paul's letters. The focus of this chapter is twofold: (1) to expand into diverse aspects of human life through the history and people, and (2) to elucidate the subjective participation of Christ (Christ's faith) within a threefold theology of Paul's gospel.

---

1. As we will see in this chapter, Christ's faith is to be understood in view of his entire earthly life that leads to his crucifixion. Paul does not ignore Jesus' earthly ministry even though his letters do not contain Jesus materials such as stories about Jesus' water baptism or public ministry. This is because Paul wrote letters, not stories about Jesus. In fact, his letters, predating the canonical gospels, convey a more vivid picture of early Jesus movement and of early Christology. Jesus' faith can be understood as "faithful obedience to God," as Paul implies in Rom 1:5. Paul states that the purpose of his mission is to bring about "the obedience of faith" (as the subjective genitive, meaning "the faithful obedience") among Gentiles.

> **EXCURSUS:** History of Faith
>
> The Hebrew word for faith is *emunah* (for example, Hab 2:4: "The one who is righteous shall live by faith"), whose basic meaning has to do with faithfulness, fidelity, or steadfastness. All of these involve a person's cost and time, as Abraham paid such a price in living his lifelong journey of steadfastness to God. In the New Testament, the Greek word for faith is *pistis*, whose basic meaning also has to do with faithfulness, fidelity, or commitment.[2] Christ was faithful to God by living out God's righteousness (Rom 3:21–26). Paul was also faithful to God by following Christ's footsteps. The believers (followers of Christ) are also required to have faithfulness like Abraham and Jesus. The Latin word for faith is *fides*, whose basic connotation has to do with trust, protection, or reliance. All of these concepts of faith have nothing to do with belief in the sense of believing whether certain things are true (cognitive agreement). Rather, faith involves both belief and action, and not once but consistently through life. One of the problems in English translation is that there is no equivalent English verb for the Greek verb *pisteuo*, whose noun is *pistis* (faith). The closest thing in English might be a form like "faithize." We translate the Greek verb *pisteuo* to "to believe" in most English versions. "To believe" is the infinitive of "belief," not of "faith." Many problems are created because of this, as it can mean accepting certain doctrines or a set of teaching rather than an ongoing trusting relationship with God. If we had the verb "faithize" in English, we could reduce the unnecessary misunderstandings regarding *pisteuo*. Even though we could translate it as "to have faith" instead of "to believe," it still does not fully correlate to the original Greek verb *pisteuo*, since there is no English verb for it. In the Deutero-Pauline and Pastoral Letters, however, the use of the same Greek words such as *pistis* or *pisteuo* is very different from that of the four Gospels and Paul's seven authentic letters. Whereas faith in the former means accepting a set of teachings, faith in the latter means trust, fidelity, or steadfastness. "To believe" can be a good translation for these later letters Deutero-Pauline and non-Pauline Pastoral Letters). We will see comparisons and contrasts of this sort of concept of faith later in this chapter.

---

2. Danker, *Greek English Lexicon*, 816–20. Brown, *BDB Hebrew English Dictionary*, 53. Stowers, *A Rereading of Romans*, 199–200. Williams, *Galatians*, 61–82.

"THE FAITH OF CHRIST" (PISTIS CHRISTOU) IN PAULINE STUDIES

"The faith of Christ" appears in Rom 3:21–26 and Gal 2:16–17. There are different opinions about the interpretation of this phrase.[3] First, "the faith of Christ" (Rom 3:23, 26) is read as the believer's faith in Christ, who made a perfect sacrifice for sinners once and for all. An individual's righteousness is possible by his or her faith accepting Christ's vicarious death (atonement), in the penal substitution or satisfaction theory. For Augustine, this individual righteousness is imputed in the sense that a sinner is declared to be innocent because of Christ's death, as a price for being justified even though he or she is not innocent. For Luther, it is imparted in the sense that a sinner is given a status of righteousness (as truly being a property of one's being). As Christ once and for all made the sacrifice, the sinner is now also guaranteed this benefit of individual righteousness.[4] This gift of individual salvation or justification is received only through faith in Christ. There is no need for the believer to make this righteousness personal other than to believe in Christ (Christ as the object of faith) or to accept Christ's atoning work. This reading emphasizes a personal salvation identity.

Second, "the faith of Christ" is read as "faith in Christ" and it makes a new community possible. Through the believer's faith in Christ, a new people of God are made. Here faith in Christ does not refer to atonement, but refers to the believer's trust in or loyalty to Christ's life. Christ mended a broken human relationship with God through his sacrifice (the role of his death as removing walls between God and humans). Now followers of Jesus are reconciled with God and sanctified by living faithfully according to the example of Christ's faith. Even though their relationship with God is secured or opened through Christ's sacrifice, the role of the believer is also important.

Third, "the faith of Christ" is read as Christ's faith (the subjective genitive) that discloses God's righteousness.[5] This reading interprets both *dikaiosyne theou* and *pistis christou* as subjective genitives. Within this reading there are several sub-readings possible, depending on the view of God's righteousness and of Christ's faith. First, if God's righteousness is

---

3. See Reasoner, *Romans in Full Circle*, 23–41. Johnson, "Rom 3:21–26 and the Faith of Jesus," 77–90. See also Hays, "*Pistis* and Pauline Christology: What is at Stake?" 53. Williams, "Again *Pistis Christou*," 431–47.

4. Jesus' one time sacrifice can be understood as one of the following atonement theories: ransom theory, penal substitution theory, or satisfaction theory. All of these theories do not emphasize Christ's faith.

5. Hays, "The Faith of Jesus Christ," 141–62.

understood as his character (such as justice, holiness), what is disclosed through Christ's faith is God's character. That is, Christ's life and death show such a character of God. Christ's life and death can be understood in light of his embodiment of God's love and justice for the world. Second, if God's righteousness is understood as covenantal faithfulness extended to all Jews and Gentiles, what is disclosed through Christ's faith is a sort of "family album" where all are welcomed in God's household. Christ's life and death can be understood in the creation of a universal and equal community. This reading is typical of the New Perspective on Paul. Third, if God's righteousness is understood as an eschatological new age breaking into history, what is disclosed through Christ's faith is new time in the now and future. In this sub-reading, Christ's faith is focused on his death, which is a decisive eschatological key that God uses to initiate a new time because of Christ's faith (dying on a cross). Through the act of Christ's obedience to the law (love) of God, God deals with the past and opens a new time so that everybody can now join through faith in God or through participation in Christ's faith. Fourth, if God's righteousness is understood as social, economic justice (and judgment included), what is disclosed through Christ's faith is a just community for all. This reading is especially true for people under oppression or suppression by evil powers or systems such as found in the Roman Empire.

A more holistic reading is one that emphasizes the subjective genitive aspect of *pistis christou* along with that of *dikaiosyne theou*. As we saw above, that reading, though varied, makes better sense to the world of Paul in which God and Messiah have active roles to play. A holistic reading puts all the sub-readings together as long as they make sense. Put differently, all possible aspects of Christ's faithfulness are to be considered in relation to God's righteousness, which was also viewed to include all aspects of God's righteousness. Second, a more holistic reading should separate the role of Christ from that of God because Jesus becomes Messiah by his faithful obedience to God. From God's perspective, that is why he is declared to be his Son. What this suggests is that there is a cost involved in becoming Messiah, a light to all people. But that is not the end of the story because even his light cannot be shown unless people are brought into it. In other words, there must be equal involvement from the believers. That is the topic of the next chapter. By way of summary, we will see how Christ's faith links with God's righteousness and the faith of those who follow him (believers).

MESSIAH IN THE HEBREW BIBLE

"Messiah" is derived from the Hebrew *mashiah*, "the anointed one." In Greek "the anointed one" is "Christ." This term is used in a variety of contexts in the Hebrew Bible. In cultic setting, the anointed ones are holy ones or priests who make sacrifices to God (Lev 4:3; 2 Sam 1:14). In the prophetic setting, prophets are anointed to serve as God's speaker in society (1 Kgs 19:16; Isa 61:1; Ps 105:15). In the national political setting, kings are anointed and serve as God's surrogates.[6] In Davidic monarchy, David is the anointed one of the Lord (Ps 2). At times, Israel as a whole is called the anointed one or God's son (Exod 4:21; Ps 2:7; Hab 3:13; Hos 11:1).[7] God wants the whole of Israel, the anointed one, to live in holiness according to God's character of holiness (Lev 17–26).

By and large, in the Hebrew Bible, the role and function of the anointed one (messiah) has to do with some kind of public, godly work. For example, anointed priests serve God and people to make reconciliation between God and the people through sacrifices. Priests help people to live holy. They are leaders of society. The prophets are the voices of God for the people and remind them to think about social justice and to maintain fair balance among them. They critique and lead the society to be healthy. Before the Davidic monarchy, Israelite life was organized and maintained around this holy office of priest and prophet. Anointment is not only a sign of God's recognition of such a ministry but also a symbol of public duty for God's people.

However, when the Davidic monarchy emerges along with stratified society, this office of priest and prophet dwindles and merges with the kingly power. Now King David becomes the sole messiah of God, who will rule the house of David forever through his descendants (2 Sam 7). The king's role as the anointed one is to maintain peace and security in his kingdom. Therefore, the ability to rule the kingdom is important. The most powerful, successful king needs the most powerful military. The Davidic monarchy makes its power structure perpetually hierarchical, placing his kingship on top, at the price of ordinary low-class people. Under this monarchy and highly stratified society, many poor people are oppressed and marginalized. Because of this hostile rule of kingship, the

---

6. Mettinger, *King and Messiah*, 185–232.

7. Surprisingly, Cyrus, king of Persia, is also called the anointed one because he allowed exiled Jews to return to Jerusalem (Isa 45:1).

eighth-century BCE prophets such as Amos and Hosea criticize this corrupt political and economic oppression (Amos 9:11; Mic 5:2). Jeremiah also criticizes the political leaders of the day for not taking care of God's people (Jer 22:30; 23:6). Zechariah presents an alternative image of a king based on humble, peaceful rule (Zech 9:9).

In sum, in the Hebrew Bible there is diverse use of the term "the anointed one" (messiah). The whole purpose of the messiah, personal or communal, is to help God's people live a life of holiness so that they can embody God's righteousness in the world. Whether in good or bad times, God's people need good messiahs because their lives need continual guidance, challenge, and empowerment. Thus the messiah is to be faithful to God's mandate of love and justice in the world.

MESSIAH IN SECOND TEMPLE JUDAISM AND DIASPORA EXPERIENCE

When the Jews returned to Jerusalem from the Babylonian exile, they attempted to reorganize their life centered on the temple with renewal of the law.[8] Ezra and Nehemiah led post-exile reform activities in Jerusalem, emphasizing purity and boundary at the sacrifice of diversity or multicultural environment.[9] During this time under Persian rule, priests or scribes gained power and functioned as God's agents. Ever since the Jewish national identity was in danger during Second Temple Judaism, the expectation of a future king like David was ingrained in their minds for a long time, aspiring for an ideal time once more in their lifetimes.[10] This idea of the future Messiah comes naturally to every generation of Jews because they need a strong leader and golden age like in the Davidic time. Though there are often competing views of the Messiah to come, the messianic expectations have never dwindled in Jewish history. In the

---

8. As discussed in the previous chapter, the exile experience of Jews in Babylon caused them to rethink about their view of God and responsibility as God's covenanted people. Before the Babylonian exile, their view of God is in a way naïve that no matter what happens God will protect them. But the reality they experience is so incongruous to their concept of God that they change their view of God to the extent that their reality is a result of their action, not solely by God.

9. Under Persian rule, Jews in Jerusalem were not settled down as they wished. Rather, there were still tensions between those who returned from exile and those who stayed in Jerusalem. Struggles for hegemony within this Jewish community continued.

10. Collins, "Pre-Christian Jewish Messianism," 1–20.

following we will see the diverse ways of expressing the Jewish Messiah during Second Temple Judaism.

Mighty Warrior Messiah (Davidic King)

The expectation of a kingly messiah is primary throughout history because David had been an ideal king for the Jews.[11] After the fall of Jerusalem by Babylon and the Jews' return to Jerusalem, some tried to rebuild a powerful monarchy like the Davidic one, which was not allowed by the Persian king. Zerubbabel attempted to be the figure of the messiah for that kingly job, and his name Zerubbabel actually means the "shoot of Babylon" (Hag 1–2; Zech 3:8; 6:12). *Psalms of Solomon*, written in the first century BCE, calls for a Davidic king to be reestablished instead of the Hasmonean rulers, who are not descendants of David. The Hasmonean rule was not well accepted by Jews because it allowed for the Greek cultural invasion into their homeland. This view of a mighty warrior messiah is being carried into the first century's religious, political landscape in Palestine.

The Divine Figure Messiah

The origin of the idea of divine messiah comes from the Hellenistic influence during the second century BCE and onward when many Jewish Pseudepigrapha were produced. Daniel was also written during the rule of the Seleucid kingdom. Through the form of an otherworldly journey, people express their concerns and hopes for a better future when they will be truly liberated from the imperial rules. In this socio-cultural milieu, the "son of man" riding on the clouds is the supernatural figure coming to judge the world (Dan 7:13–14; 8:16–18). In one of the Jewish Pseudepigrapha, the "son of man" is described as an angelic figure: "one who had a head of days, and his head was like white wool. And with him was another, whose face was like the appearance of a man; and his face was full of graciousness like one of the holy angels" (1 Enoch 46:1). The son of man in 1 Enoch is a judge sitting on the throne of glory, the anointed one (48:10; 52:4). In this writing, it is not clear whether this future eschatological figure is a king or a priest, or even a prophet.[12] However, in 4 Ezra (an apocalyptic writing from the end of the first century CE), we see the son of man connected with the Davidic messiah. This son of man, represented by the lion,

---

11. Ibid.
12. Collins, "Pre-Christian Jewish Messianism," 17.

conquers Rome, represented by the eagle (Ezra 11–13).[13] Mark 14:62 also states the son of man figure as much like Daniel and the interpretation of it will ensue later in the section of the Crucified Messiah.

Two Messiahs (Priestly and Kingly)

In the Qumran community two messiahs are expected: "the messiahs of Aaron and Israel."[14] This community, sectarian in nature, withdrew to the desert because, on one hand, the Jerusalem temple and its leadership were corrupt and, on the other hand, they needed to set up an alternative eschatological community, based on the ascetic life style and strict community rules. In this setting, the more important messiah is said to be the priestly one. In fact, this priestly community was very critical of Jerusalem's leadership and how they ran the temple. Not surprisingly, their awaited messiahs are exclusive. The Qumran community members are the only ones who are ready to receive the ultimate salvation on the last day. The benefits are reserved for those who live in this community, abiding by the rules. This kind of sectarian vision of salvation and the messiah deviates from the traditional Jewish thought rooted in the Hebrew Bible where the messiah should be for all of them. That is, the Davidic messiah will be expected to recover Israel from the foreign powers.

The Crucified Messiah

The early Christians' claim about Jesus as the Lord and messiah is a radical one from the perspective of normative Jews, because it is a scandal; no one hung on a cross can be God's messiah.[15] This claim is also foolish because the crucifixion is a source of shame and punishment. This view of the messiah is very different from the earlier views of the Jewish messiah. Christ Jesus becomes a messiah not because of his crucifixion but because of his life-risking, faithfulness to God. His crucifixion can be understood

---

13. *Sibylline Oracles* has similar thoughts about the son of man as found in 4 Ezra: for example, "a king sent from God" (5:108–109), an "exceptional man from the sky" (5:256), and "a blessed man from the expanses of heaven with a scepter in his hands which God gave him" (5:414).

14. Rule of the Community 9:11. See also Collins, "Pre-Christian Jewish Messianism," 1–20.

15. Paul inherits this view of Messiah from his fellow Christians. His letters predate the canonical gospels in the New Testament and give a more vivid picture of early Christianity that confesses that Jesus crucified is the messiah and the Lord. We will see this aspect later on in this chapter.

as a result of his faithfulness as the messiah. The view of the messiah in each canonical gospel is different with each other, but the cause of his death has to do with his message. That is, Jesus' earthly ministry ended with his crucifixion. But God vindicates his Son by resurrecting him. Thus the seeming failure of Jesus' crucifixion is not the end of the story. The canonical gospels boldly claim that his crucifixion is morally challenging, and breaks the familiar logic of success-driven theology and politics.

MESSIAH IN THE GRECO-ROMAN EMPIRES

Though the title of Christ or messiah was not used for Caesar, undoubtedly, Caesar functions as the anointed one in the Roman Empire. Augustus is the son of a god, who rules the whole world. He is the Lord (*kyrios*). Caesar is the symbol of the greatest honor and power, and does not sacrifice himself for others; rather, he sacrifices others for his power in the Empire. Caesar is faithful to his own empire, risking people under him. Caesar asks people for their faith in him whereas Christ asks people for their faith in God for others.

PAUL AND CHRIST'S FAITH

Paul, as a Diaspora Jew living in the Hellenistic culture, is familiar with the Jewish traditions about the messiah. Paul, a former Pharisee, seems to wait for a royal Davidic messiah or a powerful, prophetic leader who can lead the people to a perfect kingdom. Paul believed that such a kingdom of God could come through a renewal of the law. That is why he seeks to persecute Christian churches because the crucified one cannot be the messiah in Jewish tradition but a blasphemy to God. But Paul says he had a revelation from Christ; now he realizes "Christ crucified" is the Lord. In other words, Jesus who was crucified is indeed a messiah, not simply because he died for sinners but because he showed his faithfulness to God by dying on a cross.[16] Jesus' faithfulness is a decisive moment through which God's righteousness is disclosed, and an example through which the Christians can live to embody such a life of Christ. The faith of Jesus is a paradigm shift for Paul. Paul believes that the Jewish expectation of a new world begins with this new figure called Christ Jesus, who truly followed and showed God's righteousness to the world. What Jesus showed is the way of Christ, the way to a cross. It is not Jesus' resurrection that changes Paul's view of

16. Elliott, *Liberating Paul*, 93–180.

messiah but his faithful life leading to his crucifixion because of his love for God and his people. Again, the point is that Jesus' earthly ministry led to a cross.

CHRIST'S FAITH IN PAUL'S LETTERS

Paul's letters, though dealing with different contextual matters, amply show how Christ's faith is the key to the resolution of problems mentioned there. In the following we will see the role or aspects of Christ's faith in each letter, which makes God's righteousness a reality in the world. Since we already saw the context of each letter in the previous chapter, we will focus on specific aspects of Christ's faith only.

1 Thessalonians

The gospel of God as God's gospel calls Jews and Gentiles in Christ. This gospel is "the gospel of God" (1 Thess 2:2, 9), the gospel proclaimed by God (the subjective genitive). Now this gospel is also proclaimed and carried out by his Son, Jesus Christ. This is "the gospel of Christ" stated in 1 Thess 3:2, which can also be read as the subjective genitive (the gospel proclaimed by Jesus). Thessalonians' faith, love, and hope are rooted in Jesus Christ: "your work of faith and labor of love and steadfastness of hope in our Lord Jesus Christ" (1 Thess 1:3).

Jesus is also a model to be imitated by them (1 Thess 1:6; 2:14) because Christ suffered for others. "Christ died for us" (1 Thess 5:10) can be understood as a moral and ethical challenge to the Thessalonians so that they can live with him (Christ crucified) in all the situations that can arise (1 Thess 5:10). God's wrath is coming for those who do not live according to the gospel of God through Christ's faith. God's wrath is dealt with Christ's death but is not removed unless Christians participate in his death. God's wrath comes because people do not live up to his righteousness. The hope is that "God has destined us not for wrath for obtaining salvation through our Lord Jesus Christ, who died for us, so that whether we are awake or asleep we may live with him" (1 Thess 5:9–10). Those who live by this faith of Jesus will be rescued from God's wrath, not done away with once and for all: "to wait for his Son from heaven, whom he raised from the dead— Jesus, who rescues us from the wrath that is coming" (1 Thess 1:10).

The Thessalonians are recent converts from their pagan life and are also supposed to have continual tense relations with the mainline society, especially under the socioeconomic system of the Roman Empire. In this social, political environment, the message of Christ's faith (or the gospel of Christ), rooted in his faithful obedience to God's love and justice until dying on a cross, is a great contrast to the imperial model of faith. Aeneas, the model of piety and faith, becomes a heroic founder because he was persistent about his destiny. He could achieve his goal of the new world through both divine providence and military power. Aeneas had persistent faith in the call and destiny of Rome. He is a great model of piety and faith. The purpose of his faith is to seek his own kingdom, obtained through divine help and military power.[17]

Augustus is pictured into this model of Aeneas when Virgil wrote the epic novel *Aeneid* to help the Roman Empire (Augustus) be ideologically strong. Augustus' faith in the Roman God is strong but again it is for his own benefits at the price of countless others, through military power and divine help.[18] The ruling philosophy has a double-edged sword: by military means and divine call (providence). As the Roman God chose Augustus (Aeneas) as a sole power and leader, all people in the Empire had to obey his order. He is a divinely ordained messiah who rules the Empire with carrots and sticks. Augustus' faith comes from wealth, power, status, and a hierarchical world order in which the Roman God Jupiter is the highest. Because he is too strong, his faith cannot allow other voices challenging the status quo of the Roman Empire. In this Empire there is no justice for the lower class because Roman justice is an imperial one that supports the Empire. Slaves have no rights of justice. The best destiny for them is to serve the higher class.

But Christ's faith is unlike Caesar's. Christ died for others to save others. Christ did not seek his own kingdom but God's kingdom. In other words, Christ embodied God's righteousness. Christ is a model of faithfulness because he loved God and his people. Christ's life and death are a demonstration of his faith in God. When all seek their own glory, Christ gave up his life for others, challenging the norm of society and risking his life. All of this is done to embody God's love and justice. The Messiah crucified is both a comfort to those who suffer due to their social position and a challenge for those who seek their own power. The Messiah crucified is a counterclaim to the imperial theology of the messiah Caesar

17. Lopez, *Apostle to the Conquered*, 71–73.
18. Crossan, *In Search of Paul*, 408–9.

glorified. In this way, Christ's life and crucifixion becomes revolutionary and never before heard of.

In sum, even though there is no specific phrase *pistis christou* in this letter, we can deduce the aspects of Christ's faith from the overall logic of the letter and historical context of the Thessalonians. Christ is a prime example of faith in God, which gives them faith, hope and love, so that they can live to be worthy of God. That is the way to salvation, away from God's wrath. It is impossible that God's righteousness be experienced apart from Christ's earlier example of his faith.

Galatians

God's righteousness was not shown to the world because of human crookedness.[19] This is where Christ's faith has a role to play in this letter. Christ's faith is a primary force to make the ideal of God's righteousness in the community possible, as we see from Gal 3:28: "There is no longer Jew or Greek, there is no longer slave or free, there is no longer male and female; for all of you are one in Christ Jesus." The centerpiece of Christ's faith is deduced from "the gospel of Christ" (Gal 1:7) as Christ's gospel, which has to do with his death: "dying for our sins to set us free from the present evil age" (Gal 1:4; cf. 1 Thess 5:10). This death is not itself a purpose as if he came to die but is a result of his faith, witnessing to God's righteousness. God's righteousness for all people, made possible through a free gift from God through his promise, which started long ago with Abraham, is now readily available and shown to the world because of Christ's obedience and example of his life. That is Christ's gospel that he proclaimed for all even to death on a cross.

The death of Jesus has significance to Christians who also die like Jesus (meaning sacrificing for others). Put differently, Christian freedom is possible only when they are participating in Christ's death.[20] Gal 2:16–17 can be rightly understood in terms of that connection with Christ's

19. In Galatia God wants all people to live in love and justice, as God promised Abraham even before the law was given (Gal 3:18–21). Issues in Galatians church are manifold: Jews-gentile relation, misunderstanding about the purpose of the law, Jewish zeal about the law, ethnic boundary and the role of promise and faith. The primary contextual issue has to do with a different gospel preached after Paul left (Gal 1:6). As discussed in the previous chapter, this different gospel is Jewish-centered in nature, emphasizing specific Jewish customs or laws such as circumcision. Derivatives of this Jewish gospel are a tendency of Jewish ethnocentrism and zeal for the law (Gal 1:13; 2:5; 6:13).

20. Roetzel, *The Letters of Paul*, 133–34.

faith.[21] That is, one can live righteously (being in a right relationship with God and the world) through Christ's faith. One's righteous life is not done once and for all because of Christ's death. It is possible when Christians are challenged and comforted to rethink the cause and significance of Jesus' death from various perspectives.

This idea of death is very strong in the letter, as Paul himself says he carries "the marks of Jesus branded on my body" (6:17). Paul also says he has been crucified with Christ (2:19). Dying and living are in the present tense for Paul because Christ's death is ongoing with him. "Those who belong to Christ Jesus have crucified the flesh with its passion and desires" (5:22). The cross of Christ is more important than boasting about the flesh (6:11–13). Paul says he will never boast of anything "except the cross of our Lord Jesus Christ, by which the world has been crucified to me, and I to the world" (6:14). It is very important to correctly understand this idea of mutual crucifixion between the world and Paul in 6:14; because we can understand better what it means to be crucified with Christ and what it involves in our lives. This crucifixion originates from Christ Jesus, who is an example of faith. The world (as an object of God's love and justice) should be remodeled after Christ's faith particularly through the metaphor of his crucifixion: 1) sacrificing for others, not sacrificing others, while embodying God's righteousness, 2) criticism and challenge to those who do not live up to this spirit of sacrifice for others. "The cross of our Lord Jesus Christ" (6:14) also involves Christians (Galatians) because the transformation of the world does not happen apart from a person's co-crucifixion with the world. Co-suffering with the world is important to joining God's righteousness to the world. True transformation of the world and people come together.

With this role of Christ's faith (his crucifixion in particular), Galatians can experience the bonded unity and diversity in Christ (3:26–28). It is "in Christ" that makes the household of God possible. This "in Christ" is a principle of the community; it is also called "the law of Christ" that helps to "bear one another's burdens" (6:2).

In sum, the center of Paul's gospel in Galatians is Christ's gospel, which is based on Christ's life of faith by dying on a cross. Christ's gospel embodies God's gospel (an equivalent of God's righteousness). In Christ's gospel, the central image/metaphor used by Paul is Jesus' crucifixion,

---

21. Williams, *Galatians*, 61–82.

which serves both as the message of solidarity for those who are marginalized or outside of the Jewish boundary of God's people and as the message of judgment for those who block God's universal love and justice for all people. In this gospel, God's church (note again, it is God's church for Paul, not Christ's) is expanded to include all people and is modeled after Christ's faith. The definition of a new community is beyond ethnic or traditional law boundaries understood by the Pharisees for example. Even the law, though God's gift, is not to be a hindrance to God's gospel. As for Paul, Jesus clarified the purpose and meaning of the law or God's gospel (God's righteousness) through a universal community of justice for all. That is the power of the gospel, started with God, carried out by Jesus, and continued through the followers of Jesus, including Paul.

1 and 2 Corinthians

God's righteousness does not come to the Corinthians as if they can possess it but it is manifested to them through Christ's faith. How can this be even when we do not have *pistis christou* in these letters (1–2 Cor)? It is possible by looking at 1–2 Cor as a whole. In 1 Corinthians, the central image of Paul's message is found in Christ crucified. All sorts of problems in Corinth can be resolved if they live through the image of Christ crucified.[22] That is where Paul says I preach "only him crucified" (1 Cor 2:2). Paul advises the Corinthians to live like Christ or die like Christ. Powerful, wise people in the community often act like they are not like Christ crucified. Instead, they are already glorified and wise "in Christ." (1 Cor 1:20–25). Even spiritual gifts are used to elevate one's own power or status. There are super-apostles in the community who despise Paul's ministry of participation in Christ's suffering until the end. According to Paul, the job of the Corinthians is not done yet.

In the face of such disembodiment from Christ's body in Corinth, Paul's advice is to live Christ's death because the foolishness of the cross is a way of showing God's righteousness. The world takes pride in self-seeking glory and status at the price of the marginalized. For Jews, the cross is a sign of failure and God's curse; for Greeks (and Romans) it is

---

22. The historical context of the Corinthians church has to do with various conflicts within this community, as we know from four factions mentioned in 1 Cor 1:12. Given a majority of the Corinthians with lower social status, one of conflicts may have to do with social status or power. We also see all sorts of self-seeking ideologies in the form of spiritual elitism or material wealth or social status.

foolishness. But for Paul, the cross is the power and the wisdom of God (1 Cor 1–2). Through the power of this cross, now the Corinthians see and experience the love of God. If some of the Corinthians are marginalized or persecuted by society, they are comforted and encouraged to not submit to the power of sin or evil because they feel the grace and love of God even in the midst of hardships or suffering. For them the cross of Jesus is not a failure but a difficult truth that reveals how God's love is shown through Christ's sacrifice.

Romans

In Romans, God's gospel is about his Son, who radically carries it out until his death on a cross. God's gospel becomes a reality in the world not because he died for (instead of) sinners but because he lived for the gospel of God (Rom 3:21–26). God declares that now the new time has arrived because of his Son's faithful obedience (until dying on a cross), overlooking all sins previously committed because of Christ's faith.

There are a few aspects of Christ's faith in Romans. First, Christ's faith has to do with the building up of a new community, which is made possible through the spirit and work of self-sacrifice for others (6:6), as Christ exemplified through his faith. That is the bonding glue between the strong and the weak within a community. Members are baptized into Christ, clothed with Christ, and die with Christ. Second, Christ's faith also has to do with radical justice within and outside of the community because Christ's faith challenges injustices and self-seeking glory and power whether in religion or in politics, provincial or imperial. Justice is a concept of economic, political, and ethical justice (see the earlier note). Christians can love each other and outsiders. They cannot repay anyone evil for evil because Christ is the fulfillment (*telos*) of the law (10:4). "Christ's body" in 6:6 can be understood as Christ crucified, which then indicates Christ's life of faithful obedience to the love of God. Third, Christ's faith in Romans has a particular role to play in terms of a universal gospel for all people. In Rome, more than anything else, the issue centers on the relational matters of the Jew and Gentile.[23] Christ's example

---

23. The letter of Romans seems to be an ambassadorial letter in the sense that Paul as an ambassador of God's gospel attempts to bridge a deep gulf between Christian Gentiles and Christian Jews. We know both from the letter and historical context of Rome that there is severe conflict between Jews and Gentiles in general, Christians Jews and Gentile Christians in particular. For example, Romans 9–11 contains the thorny issues regard-

of faith in Romans is to seek welfare for all people, because all are children of God. Christ's faith is the continuation of Abraham's faith but is radically different from Abraham only because of God's radical intervention of history through Christ. Otherwise, Christ's faith in Romans is a prime example of other-centered life that led to his crucifixion.

Philippians and Philemon

In Philippians there is also a similar problem to the one found in Galatians (Phil 1:27; 3:2). The true gospel of God is not based on any laws but in the grace of God (Phil 1:7). Now Christ carries out this gospel of God, which is "the gospel of Christ" (Phil 1:27). This gospel of Christ has a double sense: the gospel about Christ (the objective genitive sense) and the gospel proclaimed by him (the subjective genitive sense). The former aspect of the gospel shows the works of Jesus Christ – his sacrifices to let the world know how much God loves all therein. The latter aspect of the gospel emphasizes Christ's own decision and work. This gospel of Christ produces "the faith of the gospel" (Phil 1:27), understood as the objective genitive (faith in the gospel). Namely, the believer's faith comes from the gospel of God in the sense that one accepts God's grace, and such a faith is assured by Christ's example of faith and sacrifice. To make this gospel of Christ possible, Jesus identified himself with the lowly person (Phil 2:6–8). Beyond Roman peace and security, true peace is possible through the imitation of Christ-like character and action (Phil 4:7).

In Philemon, the role of Christ is shown in Paul's message that he does not force Philemon to accept his plea about Onesimus. Rather, Paul's mood is voluntary, as Christ showed such a spirit in his life and ministry. Christ's faith is a prime lens through which Paul approaches Philemon. As God extended his grace to all and as Christ showed such love of God by his life and death, now Paul tries to live by that same example of Christ's faith.

---

ing the place of Israel in salvation history. While Paul vigorously rejects the Gentile claim that God abandoned Jews or nullified the law because of Jewish disobedience, he emphasizes that Israel's long awaited messiah is Christ Jesus crucified, through whom God's righteousness is decisively disclosed apart from the law. Paul also corrects Jewish boasting about the law, pointing out that the purpose of the law is to fulfill the love of neighbors. From beginning to end, faith and promise are always important.

EXCURSUS: The Role of Christ and Faith in the Deutero-Pauline and Pastoral Letters

The role of Christ in Deutero-Pauline and Pastorals is decided by what Christ has done once and for all. Since Christ offered himself once and for all "as means of redemption through his blood" (Eph 1:7; 2:13; 5:2; Col 1:14), forgiving sinners, now he is "seated at the right hand of God" (Eph 1:20-23; 4:1; 5:23). So Christ is "the image of the invisible God" (Col 1:15). Furthermore, Jesus became a universal ruler, head of the church (Col 1:18; Eph 1:22-23; 4:1; 5:23). He is "cornerstone of the household of God" (Eph 2:20). His sacrifice is a ransom (1 Tim 2:5-6); his role is a mediator between God and humankind. He is "mystery of godliness" (1 Tim 3:16). Salvation is done (2 Tim 2:10). Death was abolished (2 Tim 1:10). The role of Christ is limited to penal or substitutionary death of Jesus (particular views of atonement). Otherwise, there is no emphasis on Jesus' own faithfulness that involves his lifelong commitment to God, which costs his life. As we see here, unlike Paul's seven letters, there is no role of Christ crucified or Christ's faith that discloses God's righteousness in the world.

Likewise, the role of faith in Deutero-Pauline and Pastoral letters is very different from that of Pauline letters (seven undisputed letters). Whereas faith in Paul's letters has to do with Christ's faith and the believer's relation to it, faith in Deutero-Pauline letters and Pastoral letters has to do with a set of teaching or belief in it. The notion of faith has actually changed from a dynamic life involvement to a set of teaching. In other words, what to believe (a set of teaching or doctrine) is a primary concern. This change is understandable from the perspective of life context where false teachings are damaging a Christian community. But at the same time, with this emphasis on certain teaching the church becomes inflexible and hierarchical to the degree that it accommodates the social convention of society. There is no role of the believer in terms of participation in Christ's death or his faith. What is needed is to accept what Christ has done for them.

TABLE 3: Comparison of Faith in Paul's Undisputed Letters and the Deutero-Pauline and Pastoral Letter

Paul's Seven Undisputed Letters	Deutero-Pauline and Pastoral Letters
Pistis christou (genitive): Christ's faith Christ as the subject of faith (Rom 3:21-26; Gal 2:16-17)	*Pistis en christo* (dative): faith in Christ Christ as the object of faith (Eph 3:12; Col 1:4, 23; 2:5, 7; 1 Tim 1:13-16, 19; 2 Tim 3:15; 4:7)
Faith as participation in Christ (Rom 3:21-26; Gal 2:16-17)	Faith as a set of teaching or sound doctrine (1 Tim 1:3-5; 4:6; 2 Tim 1:5, 13)

Paul's Seven Undisputed Letters	Deutero-Pauline and Pastoral Letters
Believing into Christ (*eis christon*, Gal 2:16)	Separation between faith and works (Eph 1:15; 2:8–9; 3:12, 17; 4:5, 13; 1 Tim 2:10; 5:10; 6:8; 2 Tim 2:21; Tit 2:14)
Believer's participation into Christ Faith as dying with Christ	Faith as accepting Christ's sacrifice for sinners

Summary of Pistis Christou

Earlier, we saw that the subjective genitive reading of the *pistis christou* (Christ's faith) makes better sense than the objective genitive reading mainly because Christ's faith must be recovered in our faith. In fact, if "the faith of Christ" in Rom 3:22 ("*the righteousness of God* through *faith of Jesus Christ* for all who believe") is read as the objective genitive (faith in Christ), "for all who believe" is a needless repetition. Thus, a more natural reading of Rom 3:22 is that God's righteousness is disclosed through Christ's faith that climaxed on a cross and is then available "for all who believe." So it is through Christ's faith that people know or experience the love of God, which is none other than God's solidarity with the marginalized. God affirms such a faith of Jesus when Christ made a sacrifice for all people (Rom 3:25). Here Jesus' sacrifice is considered as *hilasterion* (as God's mercy seat on the Day of Atonement). God acknowledges his son's faithful act of love for all people.[24] Because of Christ's faith, God dealt with all the sins previously committed. At the same time, Christ's faith challenges the evil power and system of the world, religious or political. It also reveals God's justice and judgment. In the following, we will conclude the aspects of Christ's faith meant by Paul in his letters.

Christ's Faith as Obedience to the Will of God

In Paul's letters, it is always clear that Christ is the Son of God who obeys the will of God. His sonship is not separate from what he did. Because Christ obeyed the will of God, he became the Son of God, as indicated in

---

24. The NIV has a different translation of *dikaiosyne autou* as "his justice" to make sure that Christ's death satisfies God's justice like in the atonement theory of satisfaction. Accordingly, Christ's death is considered as an atoning sacrifice (*hilasterion*) for forgiving sinners. But the consistency's sake, not to mention of hermeneutically diverse meaning of *dikaiosyne*, the NIV should have it as "his righteousness."

Rom 1:4: "Declared to be Son of God with power according to the spirit of holiness by resurrection from the dead." The will of God can be understood in many different ways. But the primary character and action of God in the Hebrew Bible, as we saw before, can be understood in terms of *dikaiosyne theou* (God's righteousness), *hesed* (steadfast love), and *mispat* (justice). And because of this character, God is also understood as the faithful one who makes a covenant with Abraham and his descendants. It is no question that Paul inherits this part of Jewish tradition about God. Paul uses the term "God's righteousness" in Romans, as many scholars view it as a theme of the letter. In brief, the will of God is God's love and justice, which needs to be an everyday reality for people. Christ was obedient to this call of God.

Christ's Faith as Embodiment of God's Gospel

As related to the above, here the emphasis is Christ's embodiment of God's gospel. Through Christ's life and teaching, rooted in prophetic tradition, people see what the kingdom of God (or new age in Paul's term) looks like. Even though Paul does not directly talk about Jesus' earthly ministry unlike the canonical gospels (because he wrote letters), his view of Christ Jesus is firmly rooted in Jesus' earthly ministry. We know this from a careful reading of his letters. For instance, Paul is immersed with Christ Jesus' life of dying, as he says "I preach only him crucified" and in other places he teaches very teaching of Jesus. For example: "do not repay anyone evil for evil" (Rom 12:17). If Jesus' teaching and ministry was successful and helped the religious, political leaders of the day repent and return to God, he would not have been persecuted and killed. Put differently, Jesus' message of God's love and justice took him to a difficult road to Jerusalem, ending up with his death on a cross. As for Paul, this holistic view of Christ Jesus from his earthly ministry and his cross must be the prime lens (paradigm) through which he sees the world, God, and him.

Christ's Faith as Other-Centered Love and Justice

As related to the above, here the focus is Christ's life of other-centeredness. While most people and political, religious leaders of the day seek their own glory and power at the sacrifice of others, Jesus' life and death shows a radical challenge to the world and at the same time a ultimate hope to people in desperate need of hopeful future. This part of Christ's faith is certainly a great challenge to the imperial propaganda and all forms of ideologies that do not promote or advocate human liberation, freedom, and justice.

Christ's Faith as Life-Risking Engagement in the World

As related to the above, here the emphasis is Christ's costly engagement in the world. As we see from the gospel stories, Jesus' earthly ministry is full of the worldly engagement. From Galilee to Jerusalem, he was often welcomed but misunderstood, put to death because of his worldly engagement. Jesus' death is the cruelest form of crucifixion, which is only possible under Roman law. His death is political and religious. Paul's view of Jesus is not different from this picture of the gospels, as we saw in this chapter.

Christ's Faith as a Model of Faithfulness for the World

Christ's faith is not the sufficient condition for the success of God's gospel in the world. As we will see in the next chapter, Christ's faith is to be lived through those who follow him. Christ's faith is not in the past but should be active in the believer's mind and life. Also, God's resurrection of Christ is an assurance to people that the cross is not a failure but a holy price for love and justice.

Christ's Faith as a Basis of New Hope and Transformation

Christ is a living example of God's love and justice. Christ therefore provides a unique witness to God. God's vindication of Jesus also provides a new hope in Christ-like life and death even in the midst of life turmoil and oppositions coming from all over the world. Christ-like life and death is a model of transformation because the believer can live up to the will of God.

SUMMARY

In this chapter we saw that Christ's faith is crucial to bringing God's righteousness to the world. Christ's faith is to be understood in view of his entire earthly ministry that led to his crucifixion. In this way, Christ's faith continues the faith tradition of the Hebrew Bible whose epicenter is trusting in, and commitment to God. We also saw that Christ's faith is God's way of dealing with the world. But all these good things are not the reality of the world until the believer participates in Christ's faith. That is the topic of the next chapter: "the believer's body of Christ."

6

The Believer's "Body of Christ" (*Soma Christou*)

THIS CHAPTER DEALS WITH the last part of the threefold theology of Paul, the believer's "body of Christ." God's gospel (or God's righteousness), which has been manifested through Christ's faith, is to be an ongoing reality of the believers through their participation in Christ. The central question concerns why human participation is necessary and how it can be done. As for Paul, the importance of the believer's action is not a new idea, but he inherits this tradition from the Hebrew Bible.[1] For example, he quotes Hab 2:4 in Rom 1:18: "the righteous one shall live by faith." The purpose of this chapter is to examine and explore the believer's role in relation to God's righteousness and Christ's faith. In doing so, a peculiar approach to the believer's role comes from the genitive phrase of "the body of Christ": "You are Christ's body" (1 Cor 12:27). The body of Christ is understood as a metaphor of living: "You are Christic body."

To illustrate the importance of the believers' embodiment of Christ in Paul's letters, we will briefly visit 1 Cor 6:20: "You were bought with a price; therefore, glorify God in your body." Here, "glorifying God in your

---

1. God wants his people to walk with him: "O mortal, what is good; and what does the Lord require of you but to do justice, and to love kindness, and to walk humbly with your God?" (Mic 6:8). The blessed one is the one who daily meditates on the word of the Lord and lives by it everyday (Ps 1). Noah walked with God and so he was a righteous man (Gen 6:9). In the Hebrew Bible *halaka* (walking with God or keeping the law) is important.

body" can be understood through the language of embodiment; that now the Corinthians are to glorify God in their whole life, because the body is the locus of human life. "All things are possible" but "not all things are helpful" (1 Cor 6:12) because their bodily lives entail the consequences of the fruit of either good or evil. Their ethical lives cannot be separated from what their bodies do as a community and as individuals. Thus, Paul says: "Your body is a temple of the Holy Spirit . . . you are not your own" (1 Cor 6:19). The reason for the Corinthians' glorifying of God is that they "were bought with a price." Here the price (*time*) is not to be understood through popular atonement theories such as penal substitution or satisfaction theory in that Jesus' death is a price of individual justification. Rather, it can be understood differently through Jesus' whole life which he invested in bringing God's righteousness to the world. In this view, Jesus' death is a culmination of the price of justice from his earthly ministry. Because of this kind of price, now the Corinthian believers experience a new grace of God that worked in Christ. They are now having a new relationship with God because of Christ's sacrifice.

This idea of embodiment modeled after Christ is an interpretive key in this chapter, and will be analyzed and explored in a wide array of contexts as we did in previous chapters. To proceed, we will sketch the current scholarship related to "the body of Christ" and find roots of the idea of Christic body ranging from the Hebrew Bible to the Roman Empire. At the end of the chapter we will focus on the interpretation of "the body of Christ" in Paul's letters.

"THE BODY OF CHRIST" (*SOMA CHRISTOU*) IN PAULINE STUDIES

"The body of Christ" appears in the seven authentic letters of Paul (1 Corinthans and Romans in particular) and the Deutero-Pauline Letters. In the latter, the body of Christ is used as a metaphoric ecclesiological organism: the church is his body (Col 1:18, 24; 2:19; Eph 4:12; 5:23). But in the former, the meaning of *soma christou* is not always clear even though a majority of scholars, for example, read "you are the body of Christ" (1 Cor 12:27a) as denoting a metaphorical organism: "you constitute the body of Christ (like a community)." Certainly, it can be read that way. But this phrase can be read differently because the Greek genitive case can has multiple connotations. Besides the above typical reading of genitive, there are at least two more options. The first one is that the body of Christ can be Christ's own body (his physical or somatic entity as a whole). But with that option the statement "you are Christ's own body" does not make good sense since it is impossible to become Christ's body physically. The other option is to read this physical body of Christ metaphorically—not in the sense of an organism sense but in the sense of living. That is, "Christ's body" can mean "Christic body" (Christ-like body or Christ-like life). This kind of genitive use is called an attributive genitive. For example, "you are the sea of peace" can mean: "you are a peaceful sea." There are two steps involved here in understanding the metaphor. First, peace is a primary quality or an attribute given to sea (peaceful sea). Then, this quality of a peaceful sea is applied to a person ("you"). Eventually, the possible connotation of this statement is that "you are peaceful like the sea." We can also find these kinds of steps in "you are the body of Christ." 'The body of Christ" means "the Christ-like body" (body here connotes a somatic entity like the whole life). Thus, "you are a Christ-like body." Now this image of a Christ-like body in 1 Corinthians converges on Christ crucified or his faithfulness. If we combine all these steps and elements together, "you are a Christic body" can mean: "you are to live like Christ, following his faith or his life-risking life (which is Christ crucified)."

Therefore, it is very important that we distinguish between Paul's use of "the body of Christ" and the later letters' (Deutero-Pauline and Pastorals); otherwise, we may lose an important message of Paul's theology about the body of Christ as stated above. In Paul's letters, "the body of Christ" primarily refers to Christ's own physical body and in a derivative metaphorical meaning it also refers to a Christ-like life. Actually, Paul never put the church with the body of Christ side by side in his own letters.[2] Even in 1 Cor 12:27a, it is not the church but its members ("you") who constitute the body of Christ. This does not mean that the church is not important for Paul. On the contrary, as for Paul, the church is important but it is not referred to as Christ's body but as God's church (1 Cor 11:22). The church is God's, and Christ is working in and for it. As Christ worked for the church (a community), the members (believers) are to do the same. In a way, for Paul, the church is a result of the Christ-like life. On the flip side of this emphasis that the believers are to live like Christ is the reality that people do not live like that. This of course is not unique to Paul's time. In the next section, we will survey the traces of human problems with a focus on the human character of not wanting to break for others.

2. Käsemann, *Perspectives on Paul*, 102–21.

THE HUMAN PROBLEM IN THE HEBREW BIBLE

As we sketch the aspects of human character or human conditions portrayed in the Hebrew Bible, a good starting place is the concept of God's covenant with Abraham in Gen 15:18. With God's covenant with Abraham, the Hebrew root *karath* is used with a covenant (*karath beriyth*). *Karath* means "to cut off" or "to make a league." Thus we can put it, "cutting a covenant." We may wonder why *karath* was used while another verb could be used. Actually, *karath* does not appear in the Hebrew Bible until God makes a covenant with Abraham (Gen 15:8). In Gen 6:18, the root *qoom* is used with covenant: "I will establish my covenant." God's covenant appears after the flood when God declares that he will not destroy humanity again by flood. But the Hebrew root *qoom* means "to arise" or "to establish." Perhaps the shift from *qoom* to *karath* is significant because the Semitic root of *karath* has the meaning of "cutting off from somewhere," which may explain the nature of God's covenant. First, "cutting off" is an act of separation of God's people from others so that they might live as God's people. Abraham was called by God to live for that purpose, separated from other people to become the source of God's blessings: "all families of the earth shall be blessed through you" (Gen 12:3). Second, this "cutting off" also has to do with circumcision. Abraham and his descendants are to be circumcised of their foreskins of the flesh, which symbolically means surrendering to God, a total heteronomous mode that humans stand before God as if they were nothing or powerless. Only after this act of total dependence on God do they become God's people. Third, this "cutting off" may also have to do with sacrifices in the temple. The act of burnt offerings symbolizes an act of sacrifice of the one who offers. In this sense, sacrifices are more than cultic practices but become moments of sanctity between God and people.[3] Problems, sins, dirt, grudges, all kinds of difficulties are dealt through priestly service and sacrificial rituals. This is a community of sanctity and sacrifice,

---

3. Klawans, *Purity, Sacrifice, and the Temple*, 49–73. According to Klawans, the process of sacrifice, including the killing of animals and tossing the blood, is understood metaphorically (and symbolically) as an imitation of God. As God examines Israelites in terms of their heart, Israelites also examine sacrificial animals to see whether they are rightly prepared for God. The act of sacrifice serves as a symbolic space through which Israelites remember and reenact the calling, caring God. Klawans observes it as follows: "Ancient Israelites conceived of sacrifice not primarily as a solution to the problem of transgression but rather as a productive expression of their religious ideals and hopes: the imitation of the divinity, in order to maintain the divine presence among them" (73).

which finds the meaning of life in the breaking of their heart for God, thus making peaceful coexistence in the community.

But as we know from the Hebrew Bible, the Israelites did not come close to this ideal of a covenant community whose character is "to cut off." God's love and justice is not a reality in everyday life. The human problem is that people do not want to break their heart for God and others. People want to eat more food or meat but forget the sanctity of life lying in sacrifice or "cutting off." Animals are sacrificed and become food when they surrender to humans. Similarly, Israelites are to surrender to God in all aspects of their lives. The irony is that while the Israelites capture animals for sacrifice, they do not give their hearts to God. While people make gorgeous sacrifices along with noisy songs, they do not feel the agony of others' suffering.[4] Like an animal being burnt, their hearts needs to be burnt symbolically, because true spirituality depends on whether one can break his or her heart for God and other people in the community.

As prophets speak out, it is not sacrifice that makes God and people holy but their "broken" heart. God hates festivals and burnt offerings if there is no righteousness and justice (Amos 5:21–25). Hosea also declares: "I desire steadfast love and not sacrifice, the knowledge of God rather than burnt offerings" (Hos 6:6).[5] The Psalmist prays: "The sacrifice acceptable to God is a broken spirit; broken and contrite heart" (Ps 51).[6] At the root of David's sin lies his arrogant mind toward his people because he did not care for them. Rather, he sacrificed others for his power.

As we see here, the biggest human problem before God is that one does not feel the agony of others.[7] This is the problem of a hard heart: "If there is among you anyone in need, a member of your community in any of your towns within the land that the Lord your God is giving you, do

---

4. Ibid., 75–100.

5. See also Isa 1:10–17; 66:1–4; Jer 6:20–21; 7:21–26; Mic 6:6–8.

6. Ps 51 is an exilic lament psalm in which David's repentance is called for to restore his relationship with God and people. Thus he prays that "create in me a clean heart" and repent his sins, which is more than his adultery with Uriah's wife Bathsheba. His sins are actually deeper than that violation.

7. Moses' burning bush experience is also explained in light of the importance of solidarity with suffering people. The flames of the bush, while burning but not being burned up, symbolize the suffering of Israelites in Egypt. Looking at the burning bushes with eyes of co-suffering makes Moses' place holy. The holiness is not because of the location as such but because it is the very place where he feels and realizes the importance of his people's salvation. Moses' spot prefigures the reality of his people in Egypt.

not be hard-hearted or tight-fisted towards your needy neighbor" (Deut 15:7).[8] The problem here is not merely a lack of sharing but the state of hard-heartedness, which means that their hearts are not broken in the face of others' suffering or hardship. The hard-hearted should be broken because of other's suffering or pain. If broken, they are not only helping others but also recovering their own hearts—becoming soft-hearted as a result of breaking and connecting with God and neighbor. This is the mystery of the heart needing to break. To make the heart work, there must be breaking of it, sometimes by one's own failure or sins, at other times because of others' pain or suffering.[9] The moment of breaking is a moment in which people revisit their being in the face of God.

The story of Jonah is another example that shows the importance of the heart breaking in the face of others' misery or destiny. God wants to give an opportunity for the people of Nineveh. Obviously, they are also God's creation. The irony is that Jonah does not want to see his enemy repent and be saved. Jonah values a large leaf more than this people of Nineveh. When the ship carrying Jonah begins to break up, he prays to save himself. But his heart seemed not to break to the degree that he could sympathize with others' pain or misery. The story conveys a difficult aspect of the human condition or character: that people defy the breaking of their hearts in the face of others' suffering. When he feels his own peril on the way to Tarsis, he seeks help from God. But when others are in peril, he does not.

As we see from above examples, the human problem portrayed in the Hebrew Bible boils down to the tendency that people do not allow their hearts to break. Rather, the human tendency is to make one's heart hard with a strong wall built around it. Thus Jeremiah says: Circumcise your heart, and cut the foreskin of the heart (Jer 4:4). Similarly, the cutting of the foreskin of the heart is emphasized in Deut 10:16 and 30:6. In

---

8. Similarly, in Ps 95:8–10 the issue is hard-heartedness before God. "Do not harden your hearts" (95:8); "They are a people whose hearts go astray, and they do not regard my ways" (95:10).

9. Eli the priest is another case that shows the difficulty of feeling others' pain. Eli does not feel or understand the agony of Hannah when she prayed in the temple for long time. Hannah's silent, deep cries cannot be heard or understood by Eli. He even does not ask what happened to her. Eli simply judges that she was drunk, and advises her to go home (1 Sam 1:12–18). Hannah's husband, Elkanah, is not better than Eli since he does not seem to understand the deep pain of Hannah's misery. Elkanah thinks he is enough for her. But that is not enough for Hannah because her misery begins with childlessness.

Ps 51, a broken heart is the key to access God because it perfects sacrifice offered to God. Even God's covenant for Israelites shows that they should cut their former habits of life, rooted in hard-hearted mind toward others. God's covenant calls for a holy life, worthy of God's calling, whose aim is for all people to be blessed in the end. Covenantal partners need to maintain the cutting stage of life separated from their former habits of begrudging or having hatred toward other people. They become a new people by having their hearts broken continuously, not only because of their own failure or frailness but also because of others' pain and misery. With this heartbrokenness, they may hear the voice of the marginalized. Thus Moses reminds them in Deut 10:18: "God executes justice for the orphans, the widows, and the strangers. You were strangers too. God remembered and saved you. So you also have to treat others in the same way of kindness and welcome."

THE HUMAN PROBLEM IN SECOND TEMPLE JUDAISM AND DIASPORA EXPERIENCE

Even though this period covers more than five hundred years, from Persian rule to the Roman Empire, we can still focus on the problem of human beings not wanting to break their hearts for themselves or for others. Jewish leaders exiled in Babylon returned to Jerusalem and started to reorganize their social and religious lives. They built new walls for Jerusalem and the second temple; ironically, they also built high walls of separation between purity and impurity (Ezra 9:3–15; Neh 13:1–27). They purified their religious habits and rituals, and expelled foreign wives out of the land. While a strong state needs a clear dividing line between purity and impurity, what is sacrificed in this are the marginalized, such as foreign wives. Scapegoats blind people from breaking their hearts and from seeing the need for reconciliation through God's mercy.

When the Hasmonean dynasty was established as a result of the Maccabean revolt, the human situation became worse than before. On one hand, the Hasmonean rule accommodated to Hellenism. On the other hand, the priest system was corrupted. The hearts of rulers were hard and callous to the suffering of everyday people. In a way, this was a time of total crisis in Jewish history not because of outward invasion but because of internal corruption and hard-hearted minds. There was a lot of dysfunction in religion and society as well.

Under the Roman Empire, Jewish land was totally devastated and its resistance was intense. The suffering and pain of ordinary people was deep because of the corruption of political and religious leaders. Herodian kings were busy maintaining their own power under the protection of the Roman Empire. Local elites were cooperative with these kings for their power. From ordinary people's perspective, there was no hope that they could look to. The Jerusalem temple system was dysfunctional and its leaders fed their own bellies. There was no true sacrificial system in place—for the sacrificing of the human heart, being broken spirit and totally surrendered to God.

Even the Pharisees, while their teaching and spirit was popular among ordinary people, did not emphasize circumcision of the heart. The goal of their teaching was the renewal of ordinary Jewish life based on the renewal of Jewish law. The Pharisees had a good response to the national crisis in the way that they emphasized strong Jewish identity based on the renewal of law. But while the Pharisees' hearts were genuine, their emphasis was not on heart or on the need of breaking for others, as we see from the prophetic writings such as from Amos or Jeremiah. In sum, for the long period of Second Temple Judaism, the basic human problem of people not breaking their hearts for themselves or for others remained the same as before. Crises and the difficulties of life became worse than before.

THE HUMAN PROBLEM IN THE GRECO-ROMAN WORLD

People under the Roman Empire were exhorted to imitate an imperial way of living, based on the system of hierarchical unity. People were indoctrinated with this idea: "Do not attempt to achieve more than your social identity can offer." Everyone needs to stay where they are. The wealthy elites are to rule their minors and clients with their virtues and power. The clients under big household fathers are to serve them with honor and piety.

Sacrifices are exacted from the lower class. Since Romans share the Greek myths and the sacrificial system in their culture, the study of the Greeks is also helpful for understanding the function of sacrifices in the Roman Empire. Stanley Stowers notes that the Greek sacrifice serves to produce "social solidarity based on fragmentation" and establishes "the roles and structures of honor in the city."[10] Given this understanding of

---

10. See Stowers, "Greeks Who Sacrifice and Those Who Do Not," 308, 326.

sacrifice or myth, we can think of several functions of sacrifices in the Roman Empire. First, the emperor himself is a priest who makes sacrifices to the god who protects his empire. He is the chosen one who rules the empire with honor and power. Symbolically, he serves as a holy, sacrificial priest who can work for the people under him. But this act is part of his ruling ideology. His power and status are maintained not by voluntary services or sacrifices from the people under him but by victorious military conquests or by political tactics. His achievements are won by military, forced subjugation. Politically, this image of priest legitimates his imperial power with connection to his divine origin and calls for sacrifices throughout the empire. Diversity is allowed as long as it is in cooperation with the imperial government and does not instill rebellion.

Second, there is a division between good and bad sacrifices. While certain sacrifices are legitimate and good, others are not worthy. Good sacrifices are generally the ones done for their lords or benefactors. Those who died for the empire are considered holy sacrifices. Bad sacrifices are all the other types. For example, a slave's rebellion and death is not a holy sacrifice. As Giorgio Agamben points out, there were some people who were considered non-human waste or something unworthy of being sacrificed: refugees or slaves. They are called *homo sacer*.[11] The unholy, inhumane sacrifices of these people do not fit the imperial definition of holy sacrifice at all.

Third, the imperial image of sacrifice does not include the suffering of people. Put differently, there is no justice in mind for everyday people on the streets or in the poor barracks of the city or throughout the empire. There are numerous people who are to live with pain and injustice. Some are killed unjustly and namelessly. Their cries or anguish are treated as non-existent. But that is not right. Comedies and satires tell of such intense living pain or suffering because of so many needless sacrifices. Are these sacrifices right? The answer is a resounding no.

Fourth, there is no genuine concept of sacrifice for others under the imperial system. All works, services, or sacrifices are done in a give-and-take system. To survive well in this system, people use others for their maximum interests. This sort of logic can apply to even the lower class, not to mention to the entire society. There are rivalries even among slaves. There is no alternative that makes change in this regard in this system. All

---

11. Agamben, *Homo Sacer*, 120.

are vying for more power or a means to live. This kind of culture along with its human problem is the direct backdrop to Jesus' life and Paul's ministry, to which we now turn.

PAUL AND CHRIST'S BODY

Thus far we have made hard attempts to understand the human problem conveyed in various historical times and literature. Paul, living in this cultural milieu, where striving for more power was a norm, realized that one of the fundamental problems is not to break one's heart for oneself or others. The solution is a change of heart or a breaking of heart for others.

Christ's body (as a broken body) represents an example of breaking for others (suffering with others) through which the believer can live out the gospel of God. Since the gist of the human problem is not to break one's heart or co-suffer with others, what is needed is a radical change of heart. That is where Paul comes in to highlight the role of the believer, which is the imitation of Christ: "You are Christic body" (1 Cor 12:27). In this way, we can better understand Paul's vision based in human involvement in this threefold theological enterprise. This kind of reading that emphasizes the believer's ongoing participation in God's righteousness through Christ's faith is very different from an individual, possessive reading based on individual justification once and for all made because of Christ's sin offering for the salvation of believers. Since this breaking with others does not happen to the believer easily, there should be an endless breaking of the heart for oneself or others. Like cutting the foreskin of the heart, the believers are asked to remove their self-centered foreskin of the heart. Nothing can happen without human participation in this faith of Christ.[12]

CHRIST'S BODY IN PAUL'S LETTERS

In each letter we will examine Paul's ministry issues and the human problem of the community. Then we will see how the believer's faith of "the body of Christ" is articulated. After this, we will examine "the body of Christ" in 1 Cor 12:27 as a test case for reading it as an attributive genitive case, meaning "Christ-like body" (Christic body).

---

12. Elliott, *Liberating Paul*, 181–230.

1 Thessalonians

Thessalonians do not seem to address particular problems compared with other letters such as Galatians and 1–2 Corinthians.[13] Since this community is one of the earliest churches that Paul founded, the major issue is survival of the community in the face of hostile opposition from society. Paul's advice is to encourage this community so that they may continue in their faith, hope, and love. In doing so, he uses the body of Christ as a pastoral metaphor in how the Thessalonians should live. The clue comes from 1 Thess 5:10: "Christ died for us." Since Christ was hanged on a cross, the image of the body is horrendous to the Thessalonians. In the Roman Empire, crucifixion is used only for special kind of criminals such as slaves, but never for Roman citizens. But the image of Jesus' death is alive with the Thessalonians in a way that it shows God's love for and solidarity with them.

With the example of Christ's love and death, the Thessalonians can "encourage one another and build up each other" (5:11). The Thessalonians are to maintain good works in love and peace not only among themselves but with the whole world (5:12–13). Unlike the Roman Empire, they should "encourage the faint-hearted, help the weak, and be patient with all of them" (5:14). Actually, Christ's life of doing this work is the work of God's justice, which led him to the cross. Likewise, the believers cannot repay evil for evil, "but always seek to do good to one another and to all" (5:15). This kind of moral ethics is well beyond the Roman Empire's, in which justice means sticking to the system of imperial laws. The aim of the imperial laws is not for all (distributive justice for all) but for maintaining the status quo of society along with the imperial power system. In a hostile, hopeless world, the Thessalonians can "rejoice always" even though the world does not change fast enough, because God brings the ultimate victory to the world.

In sum, the Thessalonians' firm faith in God (1:8) through Christ-like faith and sacrifice (5:10) is the foundation of their hope now and in the future. So they can pray without ceasing (5:17). They can wait for the help of the Spirit (5:19). They are also asked to "test everything and

---

13. 1 Thessalonians is a warm letter of thanksgiving, and we do not see the particular kind of ethical problems that we see in Corinth. Mainly, the issue here has to do with pastoral matters; for example: how to live faithfully in a hostile world as newly converted persons and what to expect on the last day. Paul penned this letter to thank the Thessalonians' faithful life and encourage them to stick to it.

hold fast to what is good" (5:21). They are constantly reminded of all the ugly pictures of human problems, which are unlike the Christ-like body, his other-centered life. "Christ died for us" is a summary statement for Thessalonians.

Galatians

The reason for Paul's anger at the Galatians is because the universal gospel of God was blocked in the name of law or tradition. The most basic human problem here is a narrow definition of God's people or a dull sense of law. As we saw a few cases where hearts were not broken in the Hebrew Bible (for example: the story of Jonah or Jeremiah's sharp critique concerning circumcision), here in Galatians we see a similar kind of problem, the state of hard-hearted attitudes toward others, blocking God's universal love for all people.

With this kind of problem in Galatians, the solution is to break like Christ. That is to accept and live "the gospel of Christ" (Gal 1:7), which has to do with his sacrificial love, his broken body for all people in making God's righteousness shining upon them, flowing like a living stream, regardless of their ethnicity, culture, or lifestyle.

The Galatians need this gospel of Christ that shows his faith. To accept and live with this gospel means dying with Christ, which is the centerpiece of Paul's message in Galatians. There are a few of his own experiences of dying with Christ: "I have been crucified with Christ" (2:19); "the world has been crucified to me, and I to the world" (6:14); "for I carry the marks of Jesus branded on my body" (6:17). The Galatians are to live like Christ, meaning dying like Christ for the gospel of God for all people, Jews and Gentiles. We can name a few aspects of dying like Christ. First, the image of dying like Christ represents Christ's other-centered love and justice and his life-risking faith. So this radical, inclusive faith is to be a reality in the Galatians community and beyond it. This kind of bold faith and proclamation is a direct challenge to the status quo of the world in which not all are equally welcomed. The Roman household is selective in terms of whom to love and who are to be powerful. But God's household that Paul proclaims is radical not only in terms of quality of life (justice, peace, love) but also in terms of the scope of life, which includes all aspects of life, from personal to political. The Galatians are not to "submit to a yoke of slavery" because "Christ set us free" (Gal 5:1). All spheres of life are within God's bound.

Second, and more specifically, this dying also symbolizes the mode of solidarity for the weak and the marginalized. As Christ's suffering is co-suffering with those who suffer because of injustices or a hostile life environment, the Galatians' experience of the cross is also for others. Simply, the test here is as to whether one can break for others, whether one can relate to Christ's breaking moment on the cross.

Third, this image of dying like Christ also points to their life led by the Spirit. Those who are led by the Spirit are to put to death their fleshly desires and all forms of evil (5:16–21). "By contrast, the fruit of the Spirit is love, joy, peace, patience, kindness, generosity, faithfulness, gentleness, and self-control" (5:22–23). It is important to take note of the language of the Spirit here because it is directly related with "dying with Christ": "And those who belong to Christ Jesus have crucified the flesh with its passions and desires" (5:24). The life led by the Spirit is not different from the life dying with Christ (5:25).

Fourth, as a result of dying with Christ, what is embodied is God's love for all people. Through the crucifixion of the world "a new creation" comes (6:14–15). Paul says what ultimately matters is "neither circumcision nor uncircumcision" but a new world full of God's love and justice (6:15). That is Paul's gospel that is built on Jewish tradition but is extended certainly through Christ's faith and the believer's participation of it. This new state of the world is ongoing though it has not arrived completely yet. Thus Galatians have to continue to die with Christ and to the world to make this possible. They are to "believe into Christ" (*pisteuo eis*), not merely "believe" in him (*pisteuo en*). The former is the translation of 2:16, where the Greek preposition *eis* conveys action, whereas the latter is found in the Deutero-Pauline Letters. "Believing into Jesus" means participating in his faith for God's gospel. This sense of believing into Christ is similar to the metaphor of being baptized into Christ (3:27). As a result, a new community in Christ is possible (3:28). Therefore, the idea of "in Christ" in this verse is not to be understood only in terms of locality but more importantly in terms of the modal dative sense, like a way of life.[14] In this new community, to die is to live. When they live like that, the Galatians can love their neighbors as themselves (5:14), which is a summary of the whole law: "Bear one another's burdens, and in this way you will fulfill the law of Christ" (6:2).

---

14. Kim, *Christ's Body in Corinth*, 33.

1–2 Corinthians

The Corinthian community may be referred to as a storehouse of problems. We find here all kinds of problems, from divisions to resurrection. At the center of the problem in Corinth lies the unwillingness to break for others. For instance, at the Lord's Supper the early-comers are those who could afford their own drink and food and ate even before the lower class came to join. Early-comers did not break bread for others. That is a typical pattern of the problem that people claim their own place or power, breaking bread only for themselves. But Paul harshly critiques this scene of the Lord's Supper at Corinth because they did not share their hearts with others. This is where Paul institutes the Lord's Supper: "This is my body that is broken for you. Do this in remembrance of me" (1 Cor 11:24). Christ's broken body means more than one thing. Metaphorically, its meaning is varied. It can mean an egalitarian community of all. It can also mean his very body broken for others. So his body signifies a moral sacrifice and challenge to those who do not live like Christ. It can also mean his solidarity with the marginalized because his suffering death is not the end of the story; it is a sign of God's justice and vindication in the future. "The body of Christ" indeed speaks volumes of this message, as our life in this world is complex. When we read 1–2 Corinthians, we of course should consider all of these possibilities of meanings. In the following, we will see how "the body of Christ" is understood in terms of the Corinthians' theology and ethics.

Indeed, the image/metaphor of Christ's body permeates 1 Corinthians.[15] Paul's central message of Christ crucified is stated in the letter: "When I came to you, brothers and sisters, I did not come proclaiming the mystery of God to you in lofty words or wisdom. For I decided to know nothing among you except Jesus Christ, and him crucified" (1 Cor 2:1–2). The problem of the Corinthian church can be resolved through the living of Christ's body, which represents God's wisdom and power. The cross seems powerless or foolish to the world; but it is God's way of dealing with the world because it shows God's love and justice. That is why Paul asks the Corinthians: "Do you not know that your bodies are members of Christ? Should I therefore take the members of Christ and make them members of a prostitute? Never!" (1 Cor 6:15). Here the issue is more than about fornication; it is about the use of the body, which is "a temple of the

---

15. 1 Cor 1–4; 6:15–20; 11:23–26; 12:12–27.

Holy Spirit" (1 Cor 6:19). The Corinthians "were bought with a price"; therefore, the command is "glorify God in your body" (1 Cor 6:20). "Your bodies as members of Christ" (1 Cor 6:15) does not refer to a metaphorical organism but a metaphor of "a way of life" (like body as a holistic entity for God). There must be spiritual union with Christ ("united with his spirit"). As members (body parts) of Christ, they work together with mutual care and respect.

Similarly, in 1 Cor 11:24–26 Paul emphasizes the remembrance of Christ's death at the Lord's Supper: "'this is my body that is for you. Do this in remembrance of me.' . . . For as often as you eat this bread and drink the cup, you proclaim the Lord's death until he comes." Here, Paul clearly refers to Christ's body as broken and crucified. Eating the bread and drinking the cup not only symbolizes Jesus' death but also the very participatory death of the Eucharist attendants, because they have to remember his death (1 Cor 11:26) at the Lord's Supper. At every moment of the Lord's Supper, participants join in the death-sphere of Christ's body by remembering his holy sacrifice for others, making God's righteousness shine upon all people. There is an enormous moral challenge at this Lord's Supper. The burden is how to live dying with Christ.

In 1 Cor 12:12–27, Paul's message of the body of Christ is clear. The body of Christ is used with an analogy of the human body and is not a metaphorical organism, as commonly believed to be. The Christian community is like the human body but not like a social body metaphor as understood from Stoicism. This image and mutual relations within the body is not like the society that is built on hierarchical, forced unity. The whole point in this section (1 Cor 12:12–27) is how the Corinthian community can stick to Christ's body (not like a social body but like parts of Christ's own body) with his spirit. Imagine the real body of Christ and members attached to it. As body parts stick with each other, so it is with Christ as well. As Christ has many members in his body, any one who claims that he is attached to Christ should live for him. The Corinthian community should function like we attach to Christ. It is a matter of holism and dynamism.[16] As part of Christ's body (not a social body but

---

16. Holism is primarily found 1 Cor 6:15–20. "Glorify God in your body" (6:20). The whole body is God's sphere, which includes inside and outside the body. Dynamism is found in 1 Cor 11:23–26 in the sense that the Corinthians are to remember Jesus' death until he comes, perhaps daily or as often as possible. In other words, Christ's death should be proclaimed in their lives everyday. This is a dynamic everyday bodily life with

a metaphor of living), members of the body should devote their energy and life to Christ because they are bound together with love and solidarity. At the same time, members of a beloved community should behave as members of Christ's body (again, here members are parts of Christ's body, not a social body) by taking care of each other. This is a dynamic everyday bodily life.

In 2 Corinthians we continue to see the image of Christ's body that must be carried through the believers' life under all circumstances (2 Cor 4:8–9). The hope of the Corinthians is not to break away from the cross but always to carry "in the body the death of Jesus, so that the life of Jesus may also be made visible in our bodies" (2 Cor 4:10). A paradoxical truth is that overcoming a death-like situation is possible only through Jesus' death: "For while we live, we are always being given up to death for Jesus' sake, so that the life of Jesus may be made visible in our mortal flesh. So death is at work in us, but life in you" (2 Cor 4:11–12).

In this difficult life context, the living of Christ's death has to do with Christ's solidarity (love) with those who need God's love or mercy. As God vindicated Jesus, the sure sign of God's message is that God will make all things come to a right place in the end (1 Cor 15). Until then, living or dying like Christ is the way that God wants because that is a way of life leading up to a true life, a life full of love, peace, and justice. The living of a Christ-like life is both holistic and dynamic because the believers dedicate their whole lives to God by participating in Christ's death (equivalent to Christ's faith) in everyday life situations.

Therefore, if anyone lives like Christ, he or she may experience a new creation. Note the present tense of a new creation and being in Christ: "If anyone is in Christ, there is a new creation" (2 Cor 5:17). "In Christ" qualifies the people inside of the community who live like Christ and therefore experience a new creation, which is not completed but ongoing. "In Christ" denotes Christians' baptism into his death, being clothed with him. "So we are ambassadors for Christ, since God is making his appeal through us; we entreat you on behalf of Christ, be reconciled to God. For our sake he made him to be sin who knew no sin, so that in him we might become the righteousness of God" (2 Cor 5:20–21).

---

remembrance of Jesus' death. Initially, it seems odd that Paul always emphasizes Jesus' death rather than his resurrection. But it is not odd because Jesus' resurrection is made possible by God's power, not by Jesus' power or choice.

In sum, the hope and vision of the Corinthians can be realized through living like Christ (which means Christ's heart being broken for others). In order to break for others, they need to have "godly grief" (2 Cor 7:10), which has to do with various images such as eagerness, indignation, alarm, longing, zeal, and punishment in the community and the world. Godly grief is God-centered. If there is wrongdoing or injustice on earth, those who have godly grief cannot stay in their comfort zone. So this kind of grief will produce godly energy and commitment to correct them. Christ's death can be understood as a result of this godly grief, because the world is not run God's way.

Romans

The contextual issues in Romans have to do with relational issues: Jew-Gentile relations and Christian-pagan relations, as we saw in previous chapters. On the deep side of these issues there are the common aspects of human problem we saw elsewhere in Paul's letters: hard-hearted attitudes toward others (Jewish attitude toward Gentiles, and Gentile attitude toward Jews). Put differently, the real problem is that they do not break their hearts for themselves or for others. Because of this hard-hearted attitude, God's love and justice for all people are prevented or misunderstood. The problem that Paul talks about in Romans is universal; all failed to live up to this spirit of a broken heart, brokenness for one's own weakness and also for other's frailness.

With this kind of human problem, dying with Christ is the solution because Christ's body was broken for others. "Do you not know that all of us who have been baptized into Christ Jesus were baptized into his death?" (Rom 6:3). No dying, no life in Christ, as we read from 6:4: "Therefore we have been buried with him by baptism into death, so that, just as Christ was raised from the dead by the glory of the Father, so we too might walk in newness of life." This dying with Christ is the believer's faith in Christ (3:26). The old self is crucified so that the body of sin ("sinful body" as an attributive genitive meaning) is destroyed (6:6). Then, "we might no longer be enslaved to sin" (6:6). Being free from sin requires the death of the old self (6:7). Even Jesus' death cannot remove the power of sin unless there is a dying of this old self. This dying of the old self may be compared to a true change of heart with one's heart looking at the suffering of others. This dying of old self is also compared to David's repentance or renewal of heart. David's renewal is through "breaking of his heart" as the Psalmist sings in Ps 51: "The sacrifice acceptable to God is a broken spirit." Then what happens? We live to God, because we died to sin (Rom 6:10). "So you also must consider yourselves dead to sin and alive to God in Christ Jesus" (6:11). This verse is a strong support of a threefold theology of Paul since there are three parties involved with each other. Therefore, the believers have to present their "members to God as instruments of righteousness" (6:13). Here "members" is not a social body metaphor but a metaphor of living (holistic entity of body as a means of God's righteousness).

Dying with Christ also means "dying to the law through the body of Christ" (7:4). We can see here particular contextual issues in the Roman churches. Dying to the law does not mean the abolishment of the law, as Paul clearly rejects such an idea in 3:31. Rather, the idea must apply to a particular kind of problem in the Roman churches, which has to do with Jew-Gentile relations. Jews or Jewish Christians are boasting about the law and impose laws onto Gentile Christians. In this context, dying to the law can mean dying to a particular kind of law or practice that blocks God's righteousness from spreading to Gentiles. How do we know? The key is in "through the body of Christ." Here the body of Christ is Christ's body, reimagined through Christ crucified. Thus dying to the law through Christ's body implies Christ's challenging ministry against the Jews' narrow vision of God's kingdom and/or malpractice of it. That is what it means to die to sin. Christ died to sin to live to God (6:10). Likewise, the believers are to die to sin if the particular kind of law or boasting of it is a problem because it blocks God's righteousness for all. Ultimately, what is being tested here is whether one will live up to the law of God or the law of sin (7:26). The law of God understood as God's law—law ruled by God (subjective genitive)— has to do with "what is good" (7:21), which is similar to a list of things God wants in Mic 6:8: "O mortal, what is good; and what does the LORD require of you but to do justice, and to love kindness, and to walk humbly with your God?" God wants justice, kindness, and our walking humbly with him. The law of sin is the opposite of this law of God—law ruled by sin ("sinful body" in 6:6). The way of life and salvation is to die to the law of sin and to live to the law of God. Christ Jesus is an example of this life. Now the believers are to participate in this path. In that way, we can once again live the life intended by God as in Mic 6:8 or in Amos 5:24.

Dying with Christ also means not conforming to this world: "Be transformed by the renewing of your minds, so that you may discern what is the will of God—what is good and acceptable and perfect" (Rom 12:2). Transformation needs the renewing of the mind, which is none other than, in Paul's terms, dying with Christ or baptism into his death. Renewing produces new eyes of faith through which this world is viewed. This world is the all-powerful sphere of the Roman Empire in which there is no godly rule of justice and peace for all people. In that world the strong rule the weak; breaking others is legitimate under certain law. Some people do not have a voice there. Others are *homo sacer*, useless garbage. With this context in mind, Paul's gospel is sufficiently anti-imperial and countercultural. Not to emperors but to the God of mercies, Roman Christians are to present their bodies as "a living sacrifice, holy and acceptable to God" (12:1). Sacrifices are to be "your bodies," not others. In the Roman Empire, others are sacrificed. In this new ethic, love should be genuine, and evil should be hated (12:9). More than that, ethical instructions are thoroughly going above what is expected in society: "Bless those who persecute you. . . . but associate with the lowly. Do not repay anyone evil for evil. . . . live peaceably with all" (12:14–17). All these ethical instructions are summed up with a single command: "Love your neighbor as yourself" (13:9). "Love is the fulfilling of the law" (13:10).

Philippians/Philemon

Philippians is also basically a warm letter of thanksgiving. There are no particular kinds of ethical or community issues as we saw in Corinth. Basically, Paul's advice is pastoral and aims at strengthening the believers' faith in God through participating in Christ's death. The believer's faith comes from the gospel of God in the sense that one accepts God's grace. Christ's faith and sacrifice for God's love and justice constitutes the gospel of Christ (Phil 1:27), which is the gospel proclaimed by Christ to bring about God's righteousness in the world. Paul's prayer is that "your love may overflow more and more with knowledge and full insight to help you to determine what is best, so that on the day of Christ you may be pure and blameless" (1:9–10). In so doing, Philippians can produce "the harvest of righteousness that comes through Jesus Christ for the glory and praise of God" (1:11).

To stay in their faith, Philippians are to "believe into Christ" (*to eis auton pisteuin*) rather than merely believing in Christ. Like Gal 2:16, here in Phil 1:29 the Greek preposition *eis* (into) is used with the verb *pisteuo* (to believe) rather than the preposition *en*. The preposition *eis* may underscore the believer's participatory faith with Christ. Furthermore, that kind of faith involves suffering, same as what Paul undergoes because of Christ. Paul states in 2:1–4 how the Philippians should live:

> If then there is any encouragement in Christ, any consolation from love, any sharing in the Spirit, any compassion and sympathy, make my joy complete: be of the same mind, having the same love, being in full accord and of one mind. Do nothing from selfish ambition or conceit, but in humility regard others as better than yourselves. Let each of you look not to your own interests, but to the interests of others.

This life of Philippians is possible after Christ's faith, which is well expressed in 2:5–8:

> Let the same mind be in you that was in Christ Jesus, who, though he was in the form of God, did not regard equality with God as something to be exploited, but emptied himself, taking the form of a slave, being born in human likeness. And being found in human form, he humbled himself and became obedient to the point of death—even death on a cross.

Paul's faith is rooted in Christ's faith and helps Philippians to live the gospel of Christ. Paul says: "whatever gains I had, these I have come to regard as loss because of Christ" (3:7). Christ is everything for Paul not because all is accomplished through Christ but because all is made possible through Christ's death—his other-centered love and sacrifice. So Paul's suffering is still there with Jesus. Salvation is not done yet: "work out your salvation with fear and trembling" (2:12). Righteousness, as an expression of God's character and action, "comes through faith of Christ" (3:9). The "faith of Christ" here is Christ's faith, which displays God's righteousness in the world. This faith continues through Paul and the believers after him. Even the law is not above faith; indeed, faith is the beginning of a faith journey, as Abraham trusted in God even before the law. Even the law should work through the law of faith. Paul's former life reflects his zeal for the law, becoming a persecutor of the church (3:5–6). What was wrong with him was not because of the law itself but because of his misunderstanding about it, as if it brought a righteousness on the basis of the law without faith. Now Paul, as a follower of Christ, understands what it means to live as God's people: it is none other than living like Christ.

Therefore, Paul boldly speaks about his own life in Christ. He asks them: "join in imitating me" (3:17). The issue is how to live not as enemies of the cross of Christ but as friends of it (3:18). Those who live as enemies of the cross end up with destruction; "their god is the belly; and their glory is in their shame; their minds are set on earthly things" (3:19). Those who live as friends of the cross "rejoice in the Lord always" (4:4). "Do not worry about anything, but in everything by prayer and supplication with thanksgiving let your requests be made known to God" (4:6–7).

In Philemon, Philemon is asked to follow the way of Christ, which is basically a spirit of voluntarism and other-centered service (Phlm 1:14). As Christ served others for freedom, Onesimus needs to do the same thing. Paul asks Onesimus not as a commander but as a prisoner of Christ (1:9). Philemon needs to have brotherhood rooted in Christ and act upon it for his people. When Paul asks this, it is not by force or command from Paul, but from a voluntary spirit. Therefore, what is important to Philemon is to welcome Onesimus as a beloved brother, no longer as a slave, which means he needs a new definition of person, not based on social status but on God's love (1:8–16).

EXCURSUS: "Body of Christ" in Deutero-Pauline Letters

"Body of Christ" in Paul's letters can certainly be understood as a metaphor of "a way of life." For example in 1 Corintians, the body of Christ is Christ's body (physical body and a metaphorical body of living, a Christ-like body), which emphasizes dynamism and holism of body in Christian communities. But the same phrase in the Deutero-Pauline Letters basically refers to the church: "the church is his body, whose head is Christ" (Col 1:18, 24; Eph 5:23). In the Deutero-Pauline Letters, the body of Christ is the church; otherwise, there is no emphasis of Christ's body as Christ crucified or its direct implication to the believer's life of the Christic body. In Paul's seven authentic letters, the image of the body, whether of Christ or the believers, has to do with holistic, dynamic living in relation to God and to the world. It is the believer's living body; for example: "glorify God in your body" (1 Cor 6:20); "dying to the law through Christ's body" (Rom 7:4). But in the Deutero-Pauline Letters, the body of Christ is an object: "build up the body of Christ," compared with "you are the body of Christ" in 1 Cor 12:27. This implies that the unity-centered reading of post-Pauline churches glossed over the dynamic, holistic reading of the body of Christ in Paul's letters. The unity-centered reading is much like the

Stoic view of society: structured hierarchically and harmoniously. There must be a hierarchical unity in the church, as we see from the Pastoral Letters the emergence of hierarchical church office along with conservative social relations within the church. What is achieved through this unity-centered reading in the post-Pauline letters is the sense of internal unity in a community against the hostile world. Also, this community may be seen by outsiders to be good, not anti-social or strange to society. What is sacrificed is then a more diversity-oriented, dynamic, vital reading of the Christic body. Not surprisingly, in this life context of the post-Pauline letters the church is equal to the body of Christ, Christ's church (the head of the body is Christ). But this idea of Christ's church is strange to Paul since he always spoke of the church as God's. There is no sense of Christ's church in Paul's letters because even Christ as the Son of God works for God to bring all people into God's household. See below a contrast of the "body of Christ" between Paul's letters and post-Pauline letters.

TABLE 4: Comparison of the "Body of Christ" in Paul's Letters and the Deutero-Pauline and Pastoral Letters

Paul's seven undisputed letters	Deutero-Pauline and Pastoral Letters
As a metaphor of "living" (1 Cor 6:14–20; 12:12–27)	As a metaphor of organism (Eph 4:12; 5:23; Col 1:18, 24)
Not used with *ekklesia* side by side ("God's church" in 1 Cor 1:2)	Used with *ekklesia* side by side (Eph 4:15; Col 1:18; 2:9)
Members (*melos*) = body parts (human body analogy), 1 Cor 6:14–20; 12:12–27	Members = community members (organism) (Eph 4:12; Col 1:18)
Community = egalitarian (1 Cor 12)	Church = hierarchical (Eph 1;22–23)

"The Body of Christ" in 1 Cor 12:12–27

A typical view of the body of Christ in 1 Cor 12:12–27 is as ecclesiological organism (like a social body). 1 Cor 12:12–26 is therefore understood as addressing aspects of a unified community. "Members of body" in 12:12 is also understood as members of the community. 12:27 ("you are the body of Christ and individually members of it") is read through the metaphor of an ecclesiological organism. In that view, "you are the body of Christ" means "you constitute a community of Christ as its members." What is emphasized in this reading is a Christ-centered unity of the community.

The church in 12:28 is same as this body of Christ. But it is questionable whether Paul equates the body of Christ with the church because he never put these side by side, unlike the Deutero-Pauline Letters (for example: Col 1:18, 24; Eph 5:23). In these later epistles it is clear that the body of Christ is equated with the church whose head is Christ. Actually, it makes better sense if we look at Paul's "body of Christ" and the image of the body through a metaphor of living, as briefly sketched above. This is the alternative reading that we discuss below.

In this alternative reading, the concept of the body has to do with a way of life or holistic life as we already saw above (1 Cor 6:15–20; 11:23–26; 12:12–26). In 1 Corinthians as a whole there is a consistent image of the body (Christ or the believer) anchored in a way of living (a metaphor of living). For example, in 6:15–20, the body is a holistic entity and therefore the believers have to glorify God in their bodies. The unity of the body with Christ is not organic but spiritual. The idea of two fleshes making one flesh (Gen 2:24) emphasizes the way of life together. While "members of a prostitute" means those who live and follow like a prostitute, "members of Christ" means those who live like Christ, understanding what he wants and does. In this reading, the body is a holy space (a temple of the Holy Spirit). The body is a living space of God and the world. The body also directs holism and dynamism. "Being united with Christ" means accepting and living Christ's way of life. In 11:23–26, Christ's body is recalled with the image of a broken body ("This is my body that is broken for you"). What is to be remembered is Jesus' death.

With this sense of the body as rooted in a way of life, we can now read the body analogy of 12:12–26 in a new way, different from a typical reading of metaphorical, ecclesiological one. "One body with many members" in 12:12 can be understood like 6:15–20, apart from the social body metaphor. Now this kind of reading based in a way of life goes with "and it is with Christ" (12:13). On one hand, Paul talks about the human body as an analogy of a community, which is of course very different from the convention of Roman society in which unequal, hierarchical relations is the norm. In a Christian community all are equally important and due care and respect. On the other hand, this analogy of the human body also fits a metaphor of living ("a way of life") in the sense that because all are connected, they feel emotions together, suffering and rejoicing together. This again is a radical idea that Roman society hardly accepts.

After 12:12–26 (body talk), a decisive pithy statement (like medicine to a disease called divisions or conflict within a community) appears in 12:27: "Now you are the body of Christ and individually members of it." This statement should mean, as hinted before, "you are a Christ-like body, you are to live like Christ"; you are all individually to live for that purpose. A church as an institution is formed as a result of believers' participation in Christ's body (his life and death). The church, in 12:28, is therefore not the same as the "body of Christ" in 12:27. For Paul, the church is primarily God's assembly, never Christ's church. The issue here is not whether or not the body is the church. The more serious issue is that if we do not pay attention to Paul's body metaphor rooted in holism or dynamism ("a way of life") we lose Paul's radical theology of the embodiment of Christ. In the following we will conclude the aspects of the Christic body.

Christic Body as Witnessing of God's Righteousness

Christic body means the believer's Christ-like life. Therefore, it aims at seeking God's righteousness available for all people, as Christ embodied it at the risk of his life. The believers are to follow the same faith of Jesus so that God's righteousness may flow to all people.

Christic Body as Imitation of Christ

Christic body means Christ-like living. Therefore, the believer's goal is to seek after his life—his embodiment of God's love and justice. Christ's solidarity with the marginalized and his judgment against those who overpower them are also part of Christ's life. The believer's life of following God is not lonely because Christ is a living model. Furthermore, the believer is confident in God because God vindicated Jesus. The assurance is that the apparent failure of Jesus' life was not a failure but a costly embodiment of God's love and justice. Now God affirms his Son's faith through the victory of resurrection. In the end, the believer can follow Christ because there is a way paved already: a difficult yet true way.

Christic Body as a Form of Human Transformation

The idea of the Christic body can be used for a person's transformation, which can happen by identifying with the darkest moments of life or with the most unfortunate people. Since we reimagine the body of Christ as the crucified body of Christ, the believer's Christic body certainly includes contemplating those moments of life or those who go through such times of difficulties. In other words, Christ's cross symbolizes all kinds of internal struggles and difficulties faced by the believer. At this lowly moment of the believer's life, he or she is ready to hear a revelation coming from outside. That is a moment where the Spirit works through the weakest moments of life. The Spirit works when a person is going through nothingness, through surrender to the power of God. That is a moment when the person sees a rainbow even after a chaotic life experience. That is the moment when the person realizes that truth is not within himself or herself but in God or in others beyond himself or herself. When a person empties his or her mind in that moment because there is no hope or truth found within, that is a moment of heteronomy (rule by another). This is the time when the believer sees himself or herself in a new way, the way of feeling others' feeling, finding one's existence beyond oneself, co-suffering with others. Simply, true transformation can happen in such a lowly moment because there is a possibility of finding oneself in a new way.

Christic Body as a Moment of Heteronomy

Of course, this particular reading of Christic body does not exclude the role of the Holy Spirit, which is the mode of heteronomy (rule by another).[17] The mode of heteronomy is significant to the believer's living of Christic body because his or her own power or understanding will not break through difficulties or matters of life. The Spirit helps in one's weakness—in the heartbreaking moments of life due to one's own frailness or others' suffering. When one goes deeper in the heart, agonizing over the lowest moments of life, crying out to God, the Spirit is touched by the spirit of a person in weakness or in a heartbroken status. In terms of a threefold theology of Paul, the Holy Spirit is interchangeable with God. That is why we did not look into this. Rather, the Holy Spirit, as the Spirit of God, works in such times when a person breaks down, because through such moments one can truly be renewed in the way that one needs God, and others for that matter. The Spirit comes to help for that person who realizes their need for others and God.

---

17. The role of the Holy Spirit is not explored here in relation to Paul's threefold theology, but that does not mean that it is not important to it.

SUMMARY

We saw in this chapter that the believer's faith is in God and that the believer's life should seek after Christ's example, his faithfulness. The purpose of Christ's faithfulness and the believer's faith is the same: seeking God's righteousness and living for it. To support this idea, we investigated the metaphor of the body of Christ. We interpreted this metaphor with a new imagination of Christ crucified (a metaphor of living), which directly impacts on the meaning of 1 Cor 12:27 ("You are the body of Christ"). Paul's advice or solution to the human problem is here with the body of Christ. That is, now you have to live as Christic body: Christ-like spirit of love and justice, Christ-like sacrifice, Christly challenge to an unjust, merciless society and people. Paul, as a Jew, familiar with Jewish traditions, seems to realize that the human problem of Jews is self-centeredness—not feeling others' feelings, sacrificing others instead of cutting the foreskin of their own hearts. Paul, as a Diaspora Jew, certainly knows well that the very human problem in Roman society is that of not seeking others' welfare. In Paul's experience, both Jewish traditions and Gentile cultures (Roman society included) failed to bring in God's righteousness. The common reason is a failure of the human heart—seeking a break-proof heart that does not co-suffer with others. That is where Paul enters with a new imagination of the Christic body; the only hope is the believer's breaking of their hearts after Christ's example.

It must be said that this reading of Christic body needs the Spirit, who works through all corners of life when the believer engages God's righteousness and Christ's faithfulness as discussed in this chapter. Especially true is that the Spirit powerfully works through the most difficult life experience because that moment is the most humbling opportunity that a person feels co-humanity of others, suffering and rejoicing together. In a way, true spirituality, or what is good and acceptable to God, depends on whether we can feel this bodily, spiritual connection with others. For this what is needed is transformation and renewal: "Do not be conformed to this world but be transformed by the renewing of your mind" (Rom 12:2).

7

"Imitators" (*Mimetai*) in 1 Cor 4:16 and 11:1

A New Reading of Threefold Embodiment[1]

PAUL AND HIS LETTERS have been read variously. As during his lifetime, Paul is intensely disliked by some, and intensely loved by others, depending on their life contexts and theological perspectives.[2] When it

---

1. This chapter is a slight revision of the article published in *Horizontal Biblical Theology* 32.2 (2011).

2. In chapter 1 we reviewed the five readings of Pauline interpretation. I will rephrase them here to see a diversity of interpretation on the language of imitation in Paul's letters: (1) In a forensic salvation perspective, Paul becomes a revelatory power, a privileged special apostle, and creative doctrinal theologian. So Paul is an authority and a model to be followed (as in the Stoic model of imitation). (2) In the social-scientific or sociological approach, Paul is viewed as a skillful, realistic thinker in the matters of community, and also as a community organizer who is concerned about purity and the maintenance of it. Paul imitates society in a way, and subsequently, Paul's community also imitates the society in some respects. (3) In the New Perspective on Paul, Paul is viewed primarily as a visionary and practical missionary who follows (imitates) the God of compassion for all people, both Jews and Greeks. (4) In the apocalyptic theology approach, Paul is viewed as an apocalyptic theologian who looks for the future salvation of those within Christ followers. Paul is an authority and model to be followed so that believers are led safely to the ultimate salvation. Of course, the spectrum within this reading is wide enough and goes beyond this description. (5) In the political (ideological) approach, Paul is read as a political theologian who advocates justice, liberation, and equality between genders and classes. Interestingly, within this approach some feminist, postcolonial interpreters critique Paul for his supposed imperial, hierarchical attitude.

comes to the language of "imitation" (*mimesis*) in Paul's letters (1 Cor 4:16; 11:1; Phil 3:17; 1 Thess 1:6–7; 2:14),[3] divisions among scholars are most clearly manifest.[4] At one end of the scholarly spectrum, Paul follows a Stoic model of imitation, according to which the teacher exhorts pupils to follow him, based upon his authority established (demonstrated) by good conduct.[5] Likewise, Paul, as a teacher, father, and founder of the community, appeals for imitation of himself on the basis of his authority established by the good example of his apostleship. Thus Paul's authority is good and necessary. Paul constructs a hierarchy between God, Christ, himself, and the Corinthians, and accepts the social convention of Greco-Roman society.[6] There should be no division between himself and the Corinthians, nor among the Corinthians themselves. The ideal of Pauline community is found in the achievement of perfect harmony or concord (*homonoia*), as in Greco-Roman society at large.[7] Accordingly, Paul is viewed as an advocate of the Hellenistic ideal of unity at the expense of diversity.[8]

At the other end of the spectrum, Paul is seen as a social conservative and an obstacle to true liberation. Here the idea of imitation serves as

3. The Greek forms used for imitation in Paul's letters are as follows: *mimetai*, imitators, the plural noun of *mimetes* (1 Cor 4:16; 11:1, 1 Thess 1:6–7; 2:14); *summimetes*, co-imitator (Phil 3:17). Elsewhere in the NT the verbal form of *mimeomai* is used in 2 Thess 3:7, 9; Heb 13:7; and 3 John 1:11. In this article *mimetai* in 1 Cor 4:16 and 11:1 will be examined.

4. As mentioned above in note 1, scholarly divisions are widespread along the different readings. Some scholars view Paul as a deliberative rhetorician who seeks to unify the community by an appeal to his example. To name a few: Mitchell, *Paul and the Rhetoric of Reconciliation*; Michaelis, "*mimeomai*," 666–73. In contrast, those who see Paul as a colonial mimicry or an authoritative patriarchy are mainly feminist, postcolonial interpreters. To name a few: Marchal, *Hierarchy, Unity, and Imitation*; Polaski, *Paul and the Discourse of Power*; Castelli, Imitating Paul. Along with Laurence Welborn, I see Paul as a downtrodden apostle who defies the power of the world by submitting to God's power. Mimesis for Paul has more to do with Christ crucified. See Welborn, *Paul, the Fool of Christ*, 1–48, 99–101.

5. Mitchell, *Paul and the Rhetoric of Reconciliation*, 39–64. See also Fiore, "Paul, Exemplification, and Imitation," 228–57. Major commentaries on 1 Corinthians follow this line of thought: Thiselton, *First Corinthians*, 77–81, 166–69; Collins, *First Corinthians*, 192–95, 390–91; Barrett, *A commentary on the First Epistle to the Corinthians*, 115–56, 245–46; Fitzmyer, *First Corinthians*, 222–23; Furnish, *Theology of the First Letter to the Corinthians*, 31, 74, 100; Fee, *First Epistle to the Corinthians*, 182–88, 490.

6. Stanley, "Become Imitators of Me," 859–77.

7. Mitchell, *Paul and the Rhetoric of Reconciliation*, 68–110. See also Martin, *Corinthian Body*, 38–68.

8. Boyarin, *Radical Jew*, 49–56.

a means of control and domination of others, as post-colonial and feminist scholars have pointed out.[9] When one encounters Paul's language of "imitation" in 1 Cor. 4:16 and 11:1, one cannot suppress the suspicion that Paul engages in mimicry of an imperial voice.[10] In fact, the English usage of "imitation" casts a negative light on our daily lives: "something produced as a copy," with the connotation of a "counterfeit."[11] So Paul's exhortation to "be imitators of me, as I am of Christ" (1 Cor 11:1) is understood as a demand for sameness, an appeal to copy Paul.

On one hand, while in an authoritative position in his ministry, Paul may not necessarily be understood through the Stoic lens of imitation, as I will point out later. On the other hand, while feminist, post-colonial interpretation sheds new light on the material conditions of life under the Roman Empire, Paul may not necessarily be understood through a model of mimicry of the empire. In fact, Paul may not be portrayed in the same light by later interpreters after him.[12] For example, often Paul and his letters have been read to support an ideal of universalism at the expense of diversity or an ideal of sameness of Europe or America.[13] A long history of subjugation and colonialism, starting from the Roman Empire down to the European colonialism of the nineteenth and twentieth

---

9. See Polaski, *Paul and the Discourse of Power*, 23–51. See also Castelli, Imitating Paul, 21–33, 97–115.

10. Marchal, *Politics of Heaven*, 59–74.

11. The Merriam-Webster Dictionary defines this word as "an act or instance of imitating or something produced as a copy." http://www.merriam-webster.com/dictionary/imitation.

12. In critical interpretation the role of readers is important and necessary, as Dale Martin states: "texts do not mean; but we mean with texts." But this does not mean that any interpretation goes or that texts do not matter. The issue here is how to evaluate the value or validity of each interpretation. See Martin, *Pedagogy of the Bible*, 1–45. Daniel Patte suggests that a plausible, valid interpretation should consider three kinds of hermeneutical choices: textual choices (methods), theological choices, and contextual life choices. Patte argues that these three choices are ineluctable and simultaneously interactive with one another in any interpretation, and thus the interpreter should make explicit these choices made, and compare and contrast his/her reading with others. With this critical awareness of contextuality and ideology in interpretation, to some degree we can tell the plausible, valid interpretation vis-à-vis groundless, imbalanced interpretation. See Patte, *Gospel of Matthew*, 15–42. See also Grenholm, "Overture," 1–54.

13. According to Louis Althusser, all interpretation is ideological in the sense that "ideology represents the imaginary relationship of individuals to their real conditions of existence." Since "ideology has a material existence" (155), it is hardly denied that a unity or universalism-focused approach goes with the Western colonialism and/or the subsequent Christian mission. See Althusser, "Ideology and Ideological State Apparatuses," 153–55.

centuries, including neocolonialism in modern days, has to do with this image of Paul.

From the outset my reading takes the concept of *embodiment*—a way of life—as an alternate meaning of imitation in 1 Corinthians, which will lead to the involvement of three aspects of God, Christ, and the believer.[14] I will argue that imitation in 1 Corinthians does not mean a copy or sameness, nor a type or model to be emulated by the Corinthians. Rather, it should be understood as a way of life rooted in the image of Christ crucified, which plays a central role in the letter, deconstructing abusive, destructive powers in a community and society and reconstructing a beloved community for all.[15] What follows is, in order, an investigation of *Mimesis* in Hellenistic traditions, *Mimesis* and Paul, conceptions of imitation in scholarly interpretation, and "imitators" (*mimetai*) in 1 Cor 4:16 and 11:1, and finally a conclusion.

MIMESIS IN HELLENISTIC TRADITIONS

In Greek philosophy we observe at least two different understandings of *mimesis*, one negative and the other positive.[16] Plato uses it negatively, primarily in a cosmological sense, referring to something inferior or imperfect as compared with the original, which is invisible and perfect.[17]

---

14. De Boer, *Imitation of Paul*, 2–16, 211–16. Kathy Ehrensperger also highlights Paul's embodied life of Christ as the content of imitation. See "Be Imitators of Me as I Am of Christ," 241–61. See also her book *Paul and the Dynamics of Power*, 137–54. See Sanders, "Imitating Paul," 353–63. Sanders also similarly emphasizes that the content of imitation is Christ crucified (suffering for others). My reading attempts to show further how this embodiment language of Paul can be well explained in relation to imitation in Paul's ministry at Corinth.

15. It is important how to unpack the message of Christ crucified in 1 Corinthians. It has a twofold message of both deconstruction and reconstruction of the world and Christians (the Corinthians, including Paul). Deconstruction challenges the status quo of society and Christians so that both the world and Christians (the Corinthians) might reconstruct their lives with a new orientation of a Christ-centered, other-centered way of life. Paul is not an exception to this kind of deconstruction and reconstruction. Moreover, this message of Christ crucified does extend to the world by challenging to such a world. On the other hand, this message of Christ crucified serves as a comforting, empowering word to those oppressed and marginalized because it is wisdom and power of God (1 Cor 4). Therefore, rightly understood with this kind of interpretation, the image of Christ crucified cannot be a means of control of others. See Kim, *Christ's Body in Corinth*, 39–95.

16. Plato, *Timaeus* 38a—48e. See also Kelly, ed., "Mimesis," 233–36.

17. Ibid. See De Boer, *Imitation of Paul*, 4–5.

This world is reality (phenomenon), the *mimesis* of the pure world (idea). Likewise, Plato's view of imitation is hierarchical in that god is at the top of list of imitation: "man was made as he is in order that he might be able to imitate god."[18] By contrast, Aristotle uses *mimesis* positively in a practical, moral sense that a person is born with an ability to imitate from others or nature, as he states: "Imitation is natural to man from childhood, one of his advantages over the lower animals being this, that he is the most imitative creature in the world, and learns at first by imitation. And it is also natural for all to delight in works of imitation."[19] Interestingly, however, the former notion of imitation—of Platonic, hierarchical dualism—dominates Pauline scholarship in such a way that a hierarchy is established between God, Christ, and Paul. God represents the perfect, and appoints Christ and Paul as his special agents: Christ Jesus as "declared to be the Son of God" (Rom 1:4), and Paul as an apostle "sent neither by human commission nor from human authorities, but through Jesus Christ and God the Father, who raised him from the dead" (Gal 1:1). Jesus and Paul are given more power and authority because of their position.

In the post-Classical period, Stoic philosophers employed the concept of imitation primarily in the context of teaching. For example, Dio Chrysostom (first–second century CE) applies the language of imitation (*mimeomai*) to the teacher-pupil relationship, as he states: "Then if a follower, he would be also be a pupil [*mathetes*]. For whoever really follows anyone surely knows what that person was like, and by imitating his acts and words he tries as best he can to make himself like him. But that is precisely, it seems, what the pupil does—by imitating his teacher and paying heed to him he tries to acquire his art."[20] Even if we see here the hierarchical aspect of the teacher-pupil relationship, the use of *mimesis* is positive as long as there is a good imitation of the teacher.

However, during the Roman Empire the notion of imitation is more rigidly hierarchical to the extent that the ideology of power is served and that all subjects of the empire are required to obey to the rule of the emperor, whose epicenter is a *hierarchical unity*: the emperor on the top and slaves and foreigners on the bottom of social ladder.[21] While the lower

18. Plato, *Timaeus* 47b.
19. Aristotle, *Poetica*, 1448b.
20. Dio Chrysostom, *Discourse* 55.4–5.
21. By hierarchical imitation I mean that Stoic philosophers put the apex of imitation into god (as Cicero states that imitation is "a likeness between man and god"). By

classes are asked to imitate their superiors, who are considered higher in status and power, the upper classes are born with nobility and power. In this unequal Roman society, the idea of imitation is articulated with a philosophical hierarchy in mind. For example, Cicero places assimilation to God on the top of imitation ("a likeness between man and God"), which is only made possible by virtue, that is, "nature perfected and developed to its highest point."[22] In the Roman Empire, this kind of virtue is deemed for the upper class (rulers, philosophers, and other elites) because they are given opportunities of developing virtue through education. By contrast, most people in the empire are not given such a chance to develop virtues. Instead, they are told that they should work in their places without complaints, as Menenius's fable hints.[23]

As we see here in this larger social context of the Roman Empire, the idea of imitation inevitably recalls political, ideological propaganda that exhorts all Roman subjects to imitate (copy) *fides* ("faithfulness," Greek *pistis*).[24] From the perspective of Roman ideology, the victory and glory of the Roman Empire is a result of *fides* shown by the conquerors. What the empire says in "public transcripts"[25] is that the Roman Empire stands on both "fate and *fides*."[26] It is like saying the destiny of the empire is forever good and destined. While appreciating such fate, all subjects should show *fides* to the empire because it gives them Roman peace and security.

---

hierarchical unity I mean that unity is based on unequal participation of members in society, depending on their status. This "likeness" can be achieved through the cultivation of virtue, which is none other than education based on reason. The learned, virtuous persons rule the world, and the less intellectual, ordinary people and slaves have to serve their masters (benefactors). In this social, ideological context, hierarchical imitation is ideological apparatus for maintenance of the empire. On the top of the Roman ideological hierarchy are the upper class, who are educated with reason and are faithful (*fides*) to the power of the empire. See for example: Alexander of Aphrodisias, *Mixt.* 223.25; 224.14; Plutarch, *Stoic. Rep.* 1053F, 1054A; Seneca, *Beneficiis* 1.10.3–4; 4.27.1–3; Laertius, 7.138–39.

22. Cicero, *Laws* 1.25. See also Kooten, *Paul's Anthropology in Context*, 106.

23. Livy, *History of Rome* 2.32.8–12. See also Kim, *Christ's Body in Corinth*, 44. In the fable the teaching is that all members of society have to stick together without rebellion even if they feel unfair in matters of society.

24. Harrison, "Imitation of the Great Man in Antiquity." Harrison thoroughly investigates the imperial, civic life of the Roman Empire and suggests that Paul confronted the one-way model of imitation based on power, status, and glory of the empire.

25. Scott, *Domination and the Arts of Resistance*, 5–28.

26. Elliott, *Arrogance of Nations*, 24–55.

From the lower class's perspective, however, we can hardly take for granted that they are satisfied with the dominant ideology of imitation of and fidelity to the empire. Social life under the empire is so severe and competitive that most of people except elites barely make a living. Under a strictly stratified society along with a patron-client system, severity of survival and competition leads to a vicious cycle of their perpetual misery, which goes like this: the more competition, the more imitation; then, the more imitation, the more fierce competition. As a result, misery is intensified and perpetuated with no hopes of an outlet. Perhaps it is the empire wants this vicious cycle so that the majority of the poor or marginalized are contained.[27]

MIMESIS AND PAUL

We do not know in what extent Paul adopts the language of imitation from the Greek or Stoic traditions. Though stoicism was a dominant force of culture and philosophy in Paul's time, we cannot take for grated that he merely follows it in a rigid, hierarchical sense because Paul's texts can certainly be read as countercultural or anti-imperial. Moreover, as we saw in the Greek philosophic traditions about *mimesis*, there is no consensus on the concept of imitation. For example, Aristotle's notion of imitation is very different from Plato's, and he seems to link human moral responsibility to it, because persons can learn from close observation of others and nature. W. P. De Boer also similarly observes regarding the concept of imitation in Greek contexts: "The essence of the idea is not so much in terms of sameness, complete likeness, exact reproduction, but rather in terms of bringing to expression, representation, and portrayal."[28] Similarly, Walter Benjamin notes about the essential role of mimetic faculty in human history:

> Nature creates similarities. One need only think of mimicry. The highest capacity for producing similarities, however, is man's. His gift of seeing resemblances is nothing other than a rudiment of the powerful compulsion in former times to become and behave like something else. Perhaps there is none of his higher functions in which his mimetic faculty does not play a decisive role.[29]

27. Ibid.
28. De Boer, *Imitation of Paul*, 2.
29. Benjamin, "On the Mimetic Faculty," 333.

Following the kind of Aristotelian tradition, imitation is not a mere copy of something but an examined, articulated response to others and nature.[30] When one well observes nature and other realities in the world, he or she inevitably involves the faculty of imitation, which is a necessary part of human development. So in the same vein, Paul's thought or language of imitation could be a discourse of moral development for the Corinthians with a focus on the image of Christ crucified, as will be discussed later.[31] What is required in this kind of imitation is to closely observe Paul's life and attitude toward them, and possibly dialogue between Paul and them.[32]

Meanwhile, we cannot rule out Paul's Jewish background as an important ingredient of his thought on imitation.[33] As a Diaspora Jew, he must be familiar with the Jewish covenant theology and the Hebrew Scripture, as often he cites scripture in his letters. What is in the Hebrew Bible—Paul's scriptures? Actually, there are no specific words of imitation (*mimesis*) in it, but there are related messages of imitation in the sense of following God's character or a way of life. For example, Israelites are asked to follow God: "you shall be holy, for I am holy" (Lev 11:45). In other places, God or prophets exhort Israelites to walk with God, which means, metaphorically, the practice of God's righteousness and kindness. For example: "So now, O Israel, what does the LORD your God require of you? Only to fear the LORD your God, to walk in all his ways, to love

---

30. Ibid., 333–36.

31. What I mean by the moral development of the Corinthians is their awakening and action toward a beloved community for all, based on the deconstructive and reconstructive message of the cross (Christ crucified). Paul also participates in this development by sharing his life of embodiment with Christ crucified with the Corinthians. In my view, this moral development is done not by the deontological approach to ethical life but by the perfectionist approach. Whereas the former highlights the principle or norm of the community, the latter underscores the image of an ideal world for which the image of Christ crucified plays a central role in inviting the Corinthians to rethink their habits and to practice a Christ-like life.

32. I emphasize a critical, creative dialogue between Paul and the Corinthians. The discourse of 1 Corinthians is not a one-way communication where Paul instructs them because they are his children. Rather, it is a form of conversation through which Paul and the Corinthians engage in knowing more about "life in Christ," as it is packed with weakness or hardship in Paul's life and the Corinthians' as well. The question faced by the Corinthians and Paul is whether or not they can reorient their lives centered on Christ crucified. In this regard, the letter of 1 Corinthians must be read through this kind of a mutual process of growth in Christ.

33. Ehrensperger, "Be Imitators of Me," 241–61.

him, to serve the LORD your God with all your heart and with all your soul" (Deut 10:12; cf. 26:17; 28:9). In the Psalms, "walk" appears 166 times within 25 verses, most of which emphasize people's upright life before God. For instance, "Your steadfast love is before my eyes, and I walk in faithfulness to you" (Ps 26:3). As we see here, we can say that one of the central messages in the Hebrew Bible is to follow God's way of life, love, and justice. The image of imitation in the Hebrew Bible is a way of life—to be like God in terms of his loving character, which is same as embodiment of God's love and justice. With this central message of God's way of life, Paul may mean imitation very differently from the Stoic conception. Moreover, Paul goes beyond the traditional Jewish covenant theology by embracing Gentiles into God's people.

CONCEPTIONS OF IMITATION IN SCHOLARLY INTERPRETATION

A Rigid, Hierarchical Model of Imitation (Stoicism-Influenced Interpreters)

Since this model of conception was discussed earlier (in the opening paragraphs of this essay), a brief summary follows here. While the content of imitation is apparently example or conduct of the teacher, the implicit content of imitation is also power, status, or honor. The means of imitation is obedience or servitude (or service) to the higher power (teachers, benefactors). Similarly, the purpose of imitation is to survive or prosper, given the competitive conditions of life. In this model, hierarchy or order is given and good, as Stoics insist a hierarchical harmony or unity of the cosmos. Accordingly, heteronomy (rule by others or God) must be good.[34] So Paul is an authority set apart by God for the special Gentile mission. With this presupposition, Paul is the true founder, father, nurse, and apostle of the community he built. Thus his word and message becomes an authority to be followed; he is the norm and example not only for the Corinthians, but for all Christians.

---

34. Three modes of human existence are *autonomy* ("rule by self"), *heteronomy* ("rule by others") and *relationality* ("rule by community"; its emphasis in relational life in community). Heteronomy mostly works on religiosity, and people in that mode are dependent on God (or other mysterious experience). What is at stake is what kind of heteronomy is involved in human lives. Otherwise, heteronomy is nothing wrong by or for itself; it can be good in our religious experience, allowing God to work in and through us, or similarly allowing others to influence us. But at the same time it can be manipulative or oppressive in an abusive context. Therefore, heteronomy will be reevaluated in relation to imitation.

An Imperial, Colonial Mimicry Model
(Feminist, Post-Colonial Interpreters)

Since this model of conception was also discussed earlier, a brief summary follows. The distinguishable feature of this model vis-à-vis the previous model is an attitude of imitation. In the Stoic model, imitation is good; but in this model it is exploitive by becoming a rhetoric of control of others. Whereas the content of imitation in the Stoic model is deemed good for society and individuals, in this model it is deemed negative because the language of imitation serves as political propaganda that legitimates the control or exploitation of others. Similarly, the means and purpose of imitation is exploitive because imitation is hierarchical and unjust in this context. In this model there is a distinction between what appears to be real from the rhetoric or public speeches ("public scripts") and what does not appear in public form ("hidden transcripts").[35] Accordingly, hierarchy is negative or exploitive, and heteronomy is bad or suspicious. Paul is viewed as a skillful rhetorician who exercises his power and status to unify or dominate others (the Corinthians) by his privilege as an apostle.

An Adaptive Model of Imitation
(Sociological, Social-Scientific Interpreters)

This model takes a particular look at social dimensions of people's lives in society, in which the hostile human environment jeopardizes individuals, communities, or society as a whole. Adaptive behavior to this adverse environment is therefore needed. In this context, as Michael Taussig states, imitation has to do with "the nature that culture uses to create second nature, the faculty to copy, imitate, make models, explore difference, yield into and become Other. The wonder of mimesis lies in the copy drawing on the character and power of the original, to the point whereby the representation may even assume that character and that power."[36] The exigency of survival in a strange world is a main motif. Similarly, Adorno considers *mimesis* as a means of survival within a biological context where a weak animal, for example, adapts to its surroundings to deceive the pursuer.[37]

---

35. Scott, *Domination and the Arts of Resistance*, 5–28.
36. Taussig, *Mimesis and Alterity*, xiii.
37. Spariosu, ed., *Mimesis in Contemporary Theory*, 33–34.

Meanwhile, Robert Hamerton-Kelly takes a different angle of adaptation, one that emphasizes a contentious context of the community. Namely, Paul's language of imitation in 1 Corinthians is read through the eye of a Girardian interpretation, which illuminates: "1) A community split by rivalry into factions; 2) calls by the apostle to his readers to imitate him as he imitates Christ; 3) the self-understanding of the apostle as victim and scapegoat; and 4) the exposition of the nature of the Christian community as the body of the crucified victim."[38] In this view, imitation of Christ and Paul, identified with victim and scapegoat, becomes a means of maintaining "relative peace" in a mimetic rivalry situation.[39] Overall, in this model the content of imitation includes knowledge and skill for survival and protection in a hostile or contentious human environment. While the means of imitation is adaptation, the purpose of imitation is survival, relative peace, and prosperity. Hierarchy is a given, good or bad, and the view of heteronomy seems unclear.

By and large, the sociological, social-scientific approach to Paul's texts employs this conception of imitation. What is typically emphasized is a mode of survival in the midst of hostile environment under the Roman Empire. In this view, Paul is a strategic thinker and a skillful community organizer. So patriarchy or hierarchy is not opposed in his ministry but appropriated for serving the community. Thus, Gerd Theissen may be correct in his characterization of the Pauline community as "love patriarchalism," according to which the wealthy members play an important role in building and maintaining the community through their financial support.[40] It is Paul's strategy of adaptation that he accepts the norms of society. With this strategy, Paul's community is relieved from unnecessary tensions within and outside of the community. At the same time, Paul could forge a strongly bonded community because of this relief.[41] This kind of interpretation may cohere with Paul's social location in Hellenistic Diaspora culture under the Roman Empire, in which he may not be bothered by a culture of hierarchy or patriarchy.

---

38. Hamerton-Kelly, "Girardian Interpretation of Paul," 65–81.

39. Ibid., 65.

40. Theissen, *Social Setting of Pauline Christianity*, 36–37, 96–99, 121–40.

41. Meeks, *First Urban Christians*, 84–110. See also Horrell, *Social Ethos of the Corinthian Correspondence*, 9–53.

An Alternative Model of Imitation—Based on Christic Embodiment[42]

Overall, this model focuses on the egalitarian nature of imitation in Paul's letters. The content of imitation is "a way of life"—an embodiment of life, which cannot be copied by others once and for all, because embodiment is a life of someone with a continuous follow-up of an attitude or character of the other. The means of imitation is not obedience imposed by the higher-status persons but voluntary sacrifice and costly love, which reverses the value system of the empire and society that sacrifices others for a select group of people under the patron-client system.[43] The purpose of imitation in this model then is to promote a life of justice and love for *all* people: Greeks and Jews; Roman citizens and other subjected people.

The concept of hierarchy exists in this model too, but is a very different kind. Whereas in the Stoic model, hierarchy is understood as a basis of power and status, legitimating an obedient relationship between Paul and the Corinthians, hierarchy in this model is conceived as a basis of service in the way that it recognizes others as higher or better than oneself. Hierarchy is not focused on power or status as such, but focused on the functionary roles of the three parties in Paul's theology. God, Christ, and the believers (Paul included) work together; God's love, Christ's faithfulness, and the believers' participation in Christ flow together.[44] Therefore, hierarchy is not understood as a rigid structure or order, as in Stoicism, but is understood as the ongoing relationship between God, Christ, and believers. In a way, the relationship is characterized by a life-giving and life-sharing partnership of the three parties. This kind of partnership requires giving up oneself (self-emptying)—a mode of heteronomy (rule by others)—as Christ lived and died to embody God's love.[45] Similarly, the

---

42. Kim, *Christ's Body in Corinth*, 77.

43. Caution is that "voluntary sacrifice" does not mean condoning the evil power of the Roman Empire or any other unjust violence.

44. In my view, only after Paul, such times as in the Deutero-Pauline or Pastoral Epistles we observe the tendency of separation between Christ's faithfulness (the subjective genitive) and the believer's faith in Christ (the objective genitive). As for Paul, believers (Paul included) participate in Christ's faithfulness, which embodies at all risks God's love for the world. After Paul, his students and later Christians tend to see only Paul's faith in Christ (in the sense of the objective genitive), while losing the participatory, connectional faith between God, Christ, and believers.

45. Sarah Coakley argues that *kenosis* (self-emptying) in Christian theology, as opposed to the view of radical feminists such as Daphne Hampson, serves to empower and transform persons in the contemplation of its meaning. That is, power resides in

believer (Paul included) is to follow in the footsteps of the cross in view of God's love. Even God's love is in vain without Christ's faithfulness and believers' participation.

In this threefold relationship there is a chain of embodiment between God, Christ, and believers, as we glean from Paul's statement in Gal 2:20: And it is no longer I who live, but it is Christ who lives in me. And the life I now live in the flesh I live by faith in the Son of God, who loved me and gave himself for me." In this statement we see three parties: God who sent Christ (so there is the "Son of *God*" as Father), acting Christ in Paul's life, and Paul's living with this Christ. This chain of embodiment is not like the chain of command in a rigid, hierarchical sense, as seen in the Stoic model. Rather, as Christ embodies God's character of love at all risks and sacrifices, Paul does the same thing. Paul lives out Christ, who is sent by God. Likewise, the believer is invited to participate in this chain of embodiment.[46] We cannot separate Paul from this chain of embodiment, either; if we do so, the chain breaks down, and there is no true process of imitation. What this implies is that Paul alone cannot be even a model or an example (*typos*) for the Corinthians.[47] Equally true is that the Corinthians cannot imitate Paul unless they are also part of this chain of embodiment.

Due to this kind of threefold embodiment, imitation cannot be taken as a copy or reproduction of something, as if by copy machine. If we take the copy machine as an analogy, what makes sense, however, for our purpose is that, whenever the copy machine makes a new copy after the source paper updates, the old copy is out of date and useless because new copies are made, replacing the old ones. In the same vein, as our embodied life in the chain of God–Christ–believer moves on, new copies (new traces

---

vulnerability. See Coakley, *Powers and Submissions*, 3–39. See Hampson, "Autonomy and Heteronomy," 1–16.

46. Laurance, "Eucharist as the Imitation of Christ," 286–96. Laurance states: "This Pauline doctrine of Christian life as participation in Christ is the basis for the theology of imitation."

47. Davidson, *Typology in Scripture*, 147–90. In his discussion of 1 Cor 10:11, Davidson argues that *typikos* is not close to "example" as he states: "The word-substitution 'example' (for 'type'), employed in most modern English versions, is particularly misleading. As we have already noted, *typos* denotes far more than moral example. It refers (in Pauline writings) to a shaping, molding power" (161). Similarly, as De Boer notes, *typos* in the New Testament is used with the diversity of connotations: a mark, a typological use, and a pattern for human conduct (*Imitation of Paul*, 17–23).

of life) replace the old ones. There will be no permanent copy made once and for all, because our lives keep moving on. At the same time, nobody, including Paul, can be a permanent source that is not subject to change or update. In this regard, this chain of embodiment of three parties (God, Christ, believer) must be a continual feeding process in which believers (and Paul) have to update their source. Likewise, a way of life in God and Christ means a continual process of dying and living with Christ: "You also must consider yourselves dead to sin *and* alive to God in Christ Jesus" (Rom 6:11).

In this sense of chain embodiment and its continual process on the believer's life, the language of imitation in 1 Cor 4:16 and 11:1 is not a rigid one-way exhortation, as in deliberative rhetoric in the Greco-Roman world, which appeals to hierarchical obedience and unity.[48] But this exhortation is close to an invitational challenge to the Corinthians (and vice versa, to Paul too) so that they might rethink their lives with a focus on this threefold embodiment, including their relationship to Paul. At the heart of this new language of embodiment for the Corinthians is a deconstructive message of Christ crucified, which challenges the view of honor/power/status-driven imitation, a characteristic of Stoicism and the Roman Empire. That is, Paul's authority or power does not come from his own personhood but from God (1 Cor 1:1; Gal 1:1; Rom 1:1). The God of love and justice declares Christ crucified as the Son of God, who manifests faithfulness to God in the world. Paul is one of the witnesses that also live through this chain of embodiment, dying on the cross everyday in the Roman world. Read in this way, Paul is hardly a colonialist or a controller of the community. Similarly, Paul may not be an advocate of unity based on Stoic *homonoia*.

Similarly, Marcus Borg and John Dominic Crossan, in their recent book *The First Paul*, argue that the first Paul (portrayed in his undisputed letters) is not the same as the later Paul domesticated by later interpreters (in the Deutero-Pauline and Pastoral Letters).[49] There is a clear message in this book that Paul's theology of Christ crucified has to do with God's love for all people, and that the language of imitation is based on Paul's passion or embodiment for a just world. Similarly, Laurence Welborn, in his book *Paul, the Fool of Christ*, argues that Paul's embodiment theology of Christ

---

48. Welborn, *Paul, the Fool of Christ*, 89–90.

49. Borg, *The First Paul*, 93–121. See also Sanders, "Imitating Paul," 353–63. Ehrensperger, "Be Imitators of Me," 241–61.

crucified is well understood through the mime: "The mime was by definition 'an imitation of life,' and took as its subject matter the coarse reality of everyday existence among the urban lower classes."[50] Welborn goes on to argue that Paul's self-description of himself as "the fool of Christ" serves as a countercultural, subversive message to those who think they are wise.[51] Paul's embodiment theology is expressed with *Christic* body (an attributive genitive, like "the body of sin" in Rom 6:6 as "sinful body") rather than the body as a community of Christ (an objective genitive, like social body).[52] This *Christic* body is reimagined through Christ crucified.

"IMITATORS" (MIMETAI) IN 1 COR 4:16 AND 11:1

The Context of the Corinthian Community

We have to begin by understanding the issues at Corinth because the language of imitation ineluctably involves the historical, theological context of the Corinthian community.[53] Our departure point will be on the issue of "divisions" mentioned in 1 Cor 1:11–13. Here one of the interpretive issues is the number of factions, three or four (Paul's, Apollo's, Cephas's, and Christ's). Many scholars consider Christ's party not a faction of divisions but a true party of Christian followers, unlike the previously mentioned three factions. According to these scholars, the cause of divisions is that the Corinthians did not stick to Christ's teaching (or Christ's party), and that they were not united in one body like the social body. Accordingly, *memeristai* in verse 13 is treated as the passive voice: "Has Christ been divided?" So the anticipated answer out of this rhetorical question is "no," as Christ as the social body cannot be divided. However, as David Odell-Scott argues, this Christ's party is also one of the factions whose origin has to do with James, Jesus' brother in Jerusalem.[54] According to Odell-Scott, *memeristai* in verse 13 is treated as the middle voice: "Has Christ distributed himself?" So the anticipated answer from this rhetorical question is also "no," but its implication is very different. That is, this rhetorical question can be a critique of Christ's party, as the rhetorical question "Was Paul crucified for you?" is a critique of Paul's party. With

50. Welborn, *Paul, the Fool of Christ*, 36.
51. Ibid., 1–48.
52. Kim, *Christ's Body in Corinth*, 67.
53. Ibid., 55–56.
54. Odell-Scott, *Paul's Critique of Theocracy*, 33–43.

this middle voice translation, the critique of Christ's party goes like this: "Did Christ exercise his power and give it to you?" In addition, we see here with this translation that Christ serves as an actor rather than as a mere object, which insinuates the existence of a faction named Christ.[55] It is not an accident that we find a group of people who exercise their wisdom and power in the name of Christ, as we read in 4:7–8: "And if you received it, why do you boast as if it were not a gift? Already you have all you want! Already you have become rich! Quite apart from us you have become kings! Indeed, I wish that you had become kings, so that we might be kings with you!" In contrast, Paul's response and attitude towards life is very different from them; it is a way of life in which Christ is crucified: "We are fools for the sake of Christ, but you are wise in Christ. We are weak, but you are strong. You are held in honor, but we in disrepute.... When slandered, we speak kindly. We have become like the rubbish of the world, the dregs of all things, to this very day" (4:10–13).[56]

As seen above, a brief analysis of the Corinthian context has much to say about the "ways of life" in Christ.[57] The issue is not the lack of knowledge or teaching about Christ but a lack of Christ-like life and death. In other words, what is at stake is how one can live being identified with Christ crucified. Seen this way, the primary cause of divisions, including all kinds of problems stated in 1 Corinthians, is not a mere lack of unity in Christ as if people could have the same mind (in the sense of hegemonic unity, as in Stoicism) but a lack of respect on the part of the members, who should embody or imitate Christ-like life and death.[58] In this regard,

---

55. Ibid.

56. Welborn, *Paul, the Fool of Christ*, 99–101.

57. The famous phrase "in Christ" (*en christo*) in Paul's letters (Gal 3:28 for example) and 1 Cor in particular (1 Cor 3:23; 15:22 for example) should not be understood only as a boundary marker. In fact, Greek dative case (like "in" in English) connotes several things: "spatial relationships, instrumental relationships, temporal relationships or modal relationships." See Kim, *Christ's Body in Corinth*, 33. While spatial relationships concern space (community) of believers because of Christ ("sense of belonging"), instrumental relationships emphasize the role of Christ on believers' community. Temporal relationships involve matters of time for the community because of Christ, including eschatological time. Modal relationships deal with circumstances or manner of believers because of Christ.

58. Kim, *Christ's Body in Corinth*, 54–63. Problems found in 1 Cor include sexual immorality (chs. 5–6), marriage-related matters (7:1), eating of meat sacrificed to idols (ch. 8, 10), rights of Paul (ch. 9), women's head covering (11:1–16), the Lord's Supper (11:17–34), and resurrection (ch. 15).

the language of unity in 1 Cor 1:10 "that all of you be in agreement and that there be no divisions among you, but that you *be united in the same mind and the same purpose*," is not to be understood as through a rhetoric of *homonoia* in Stoicism, whose goal is to unify society at the expense of diversity, freedom and justice.[59] Rather, unity in 1 Cor 1:10 is understood differently if the same mind and the same purpose are focused on the image of Christ crucified, a radical new way of life, as discussed before. This "new way of life" rooted in Christ crucified both deconstructs any human tendency of unification and reconstructs self, community, and the world in this new fashion, as Paul states: "For I decided to know nothing among you except Jesus Christ, and him crucified" (1 Cor 2:2).

"Imitation" in the Discursive Figurative Structure of 1 Corinthians

If disembodiment of Christ is a main cause of the problems in 1 Corinthians, the solution is to help the Corinthians embody Christ. Embodying Christ means living and dying like Christ, which is well expressed in the figure of Christ crucified.[60] This figure of Christ crucified is the backbone of the metaphor of "the body of Christ" (*soma christou*), which is understood as *Christic* body (an attributive genitive), a metaphor of living or a way of life, rather than a metaphor of an ecclesiological body belonging to Christ.[61] The Christic body is then none other than a way of life rooted in Christ's sacrifice and love. In the Corinthian context as stated earlier, the language of imitation means to live Christ's way of life, which is markedly different from ways of the world—the system of coercive control of others. So "imitators" in 1 Cor 4:16 and 11:1 must be understood with this interpretive frame and historical context in Corinth. In order to understand the context and message of imitation clearer, we will examine 1 Corinthians as a whole, in which we can catch the movement of the body figure alongside of the implicated message of imitation in the whole letter. In this regard, the discursive structure of 1 Corinthians is reproduced below.[62]

---

59. Ibid., 4.
60. Ibid., 65–95.
61. Ibid.
62. Ibid., 71–73.

Outline of the Discursive Figurative Structure of 1 Corinthians

1:1–17 Paul, Apostle of Christ Jesus, and the Corinthians, Sanctified in Christ Jesus
- A 1:1–9 Called as apostle of Christ and called as partners of Christ
- A' 1:10–17 United in the gospel of "the cross of Christ" and its power

1:18—4:21 The Cross as God's Power, Exemplified by the Corinthians and Embodied by Paul
- A 1:18–31 The cross, God's wisdom and power
  - x 1:18–25 Christ crucified, the power of God, and the wisdom of the world
  - x' 1:26–31 The Corinthians chosen by God through Christ crucified
- B 2:1—4:7 Paul's Faith in Christ crucified
  - x 2:1–16 Paul's endeavor to embody Christ crucified in his ministry
  - y 3:1–15 The cross as the foundation of the community
  - x' 3:16—4:7 The Corinthians' failure to embody Christ crucified
- A' 4:8–21 Paul's embodying Christ crucified, a model for the Corinthians

5:1—11:34 The Corinthians' Failure to Embody Christ Crucified; Paul's Exhortation to the Corinthians Calling for Participation in Christ Crucified
- A 5:1—6:20 The Corinthians' failure to live Christ crucified
  - x 5:1–13 Sexual immorality as a case of failure
  - y 6:1–11 Lawsuit among believers as a case of failure
  - x' 6:12–20 Solution: "live Christ crucified as members of Christ"
- B 7:1—8:13 Paul's advice to the Corinthians who do not embody Christ crucified in their social and community life
  - x 7:1–40 "Remain with God" in the calling of God as a slave of Christ, not as slaves of human beings
  - x' 8:1–13 Christ "died" for all in the community; Paul's embodiment of Christ crucified through self-control (not eating meat)

C   9:1-22 Paul's living Christ crucified by becoming weak
  B' 9:23—11:1 Paul's exhortation calling for participation in Christ crucified
  A' 11:2-34 Community worship and the Lord's Supper through participating in Christ crucified
       x   11:2-16 Egalitarian worship service
       x' 11:17-34 Proclaiming and participating in Christ crucified

12:1—15:11 Exhortation: The Corinthian Body as Christic Embodiment
  A   12:1-30 Diversity in the Corinthian body (gifts, services, activities), baptized into one body; the Corinthians as Christic body, Christic embodiment
       x   12:1-3 Jesus as Lord
       y   12:4-11 Gifts of the Spirit for all (equals)
       x' 12:12-30 In order to be the "body of Christ," crucified for "others"
  B   12:31—13:13 The Corinthians as loving body
  A' 14:1—15:11 The Corinthians called to build a loving community
       x   14:1-19 In order to be the "body of Christ," pursue love and build up a community
       y   14:20-40 Gifts of the Spirit for all (equals): a hymn, a lesson, a revelation, a tongue, an interpretation
       x' 15:1-11 Christ as Lord, died and raised for us

15:12-58 As Christ Crucified Was Raised, So the Crucified Body of Christians Will Be Raised
  A   15:12-20 Christ crucified has been raised from the dead
  B   15:21-49 The power of the resurrected Christ at work for all the children of Adam (not merely believers), since the crucified and risen Christ is the new Adam
  A' 15:50-58 A new kind of body; imperishable (after crucified death) for the "body of Christ"

16:1-24 Conclusion
  A   16:1-4 Show your love of the Christ crucified: collection for the saints
  A' 16:5-24 Corinthians, stand firm in your faith

As seen in this outline, imitation appears in 4:16 and 11:1. The former ("I appeal to you, then, be imitators of me") belongs to the unit 1:18—4:21, "The Cross as God's Power, Exemplified by the Corinthians and Embodied by Paul," and also to the subunit A' (4:8–21), "Paul's embodiment of Christ crucified, a model for the Corinthians." In 1:18—4:21 Paul compares and contrasts the wisdom of the world with that of God, which looks foolish but manifests as true power through the cross (Christ crucified). This message of the cross is a message of reversal of the worldly wisdom that sacrifices others without their own sacrifice. It is Christ's faithfulness to God that shames and challenges the power and wisdom of the world.

If the message of Christ crucified is taken as a deconstructive symbol, then the message of imitation in 4:16 does not mean to copy of him, be it his character or example, but reminds the Corinthians of a new way of life centered on the deconstructive, reconstructive message of the cross. What is deconstructed is not only the Corinthians' self-seeking power or glory but also Paul's self-understanding of who he is—a sense of his new identity formed and reformed through his own cross ("I die everyday," 15:31). Likely, Paul considers himself *nothing*: "For I am the least of the apostles, unfit to be called an apostle" (15:9). The message of deconstruction actually goes beyond the Corinthian community and Paul because it is God's power and wisdom that concerns the whole world. Simultaneously, this kind of deconstruction begins a reconstruction of a new beloved community for all. However, the Corinthians do not go through this process of de(re)construction; they fail in embodying Christ crucified (3:16—4:7, "Corinthians' failure to embody Christ crucified"). This problem of disembodiment is addressed in the next subunit, 4:8–21; the solution is the life of *Christic* embodiment.

Imitation also appears in 11:1, which belongs to the unit 5:1—11:34, "The Corinthians' Failure to Embody Christ crucified; Paul's Exhortation to the Corinthians Calling for Participation in Christ Crucified," and also to the subunit 9:23—11:1, "Paul's Exhortation Calling for Participation in Christ crucified." This unit 5:1—11:34 shows specific cases of the Corinthians' disembodiment of Christ, ranging from sexual immorality to eating food offered to idols and the Lord's Supper. In each case the solution is offered in the form of *Christic* embodiment. For example, in the case of food offered to idols there were some concerns about the community; some eat food offered to idols while others do not eat it. Here Paul's solution does not follow the Stoic model of *homonoia*, which seeks one rigid answer based upon a rigid hierarchical unity at the sacrifice of diversity, freedom, or justice. If Paul had followed a model of Stoic unity, Paul's advice could have been an answer with a single option: "The Corinthians can eat anything since all food is clean, God-given." But Paul's advice is different. His suggestion is not to seek such a unity by unifying all their views with one option. Instead, Paul stands with those who are weak even though their understanding or knowledge is not correct or mature. The answer looks to the position of the weak, which is unlike the Stoic model of society. As Christ lived and died for others, for Paul, the criteria of good Christian life lies in this attitude of other-centered life. For this goal, Paul advises that the Corinthians sacrifice their power, status, or knowledge for the welfare of others, especially for their weak members (9:1–22, "Paul's Living Christ Crucified by Becoming Weak"). Then 12:1—15:11 follows: "Exhortation: The Corinthian Body as *Christic* Embodiment." Here we see the community spirit of how to use gifts in the community.

Overall, as we see in this discursive structure, the language of embodiment is relational: from God's love to Christ's faithfulness to Paul and the believers. It is a chain of life or embodiment, not the chain of command based in status or authority. Paul alone is not an authority or model. So "be imitators of me as I am of Christ" (1 11:1) is the language of this relational chain of embodiment, as Paul underscores his relational life with Christ ("as I am of Christ"). For Paul, there is no theology or ethics possible without this threefold embodiment between God, Christ, and and the believer. This threefold language of embodiment in 1 Corinthians is hardly found in Hebrews, the Deutero-Pauline or Pastoral Epistles. Taking faith for example, faith in Paul's undisputed letters has to do with Christ's faithfulness (the subjective genitive of *pistis christou*; Gal 2:16; Rom 3:22) and believers' participation in it. Even if *pistis christou* does not appear in 1 Corinthians, as shown earlier, it is closely associated with the image of Christ crucified, which is the apex of Christ's faithfulness. On the contrary, faith in Heb 13:7 is an object—"imitate their faith" (*mimeisthe ten pistin*)—and is not directly related to Christ, as compared with Paul's letters. Faith also refers to a teaching or set of doctrines (Eph 4:13; 6:16; 1 Tim 1:4–5, 19). Moreover, faith is a believers' confidence, conviction, or assurance rather than their relation or participation in Christ's faithfulness and God's love (Heb 11:1; Eph 3:12; Col 1:23; 2:5, 7). Ultimately, the believer's faith is none other than the living of the Christic body (1 Cor 12:27).

SUMMARY

Some may still wonder whether the image of Christ crucified is a rhetoric of persuasion and/or control of others through which Paul seeks to unify the community at the expense of diversity. The heart of the interpretive issue is how to unpack the meaning of Christ crucified in Corinth, and under the Roman Empire. In other words, the language of imitation inevitably involves the meaning of Christ crucified, which deconstructs and reconstructs the world and Paul's ministry. Likewise, imitation cannot be separated from a bold message of Christ crucified as such, and cannot be taken as a one-way path, but instead as a dedicated partnership of three parties (God, Christ, and the believer).

Still, other scholars may raise concerns about hierarchy and heteronomy, generally viewed as an obstacle to human equality and liberation. In this chapter I have tried to defend that the concept of hierarchy employed in 1 Corinthians is positive. If hierarchy is understood as recognizing the higher place of others and God, and if heteronomy is understood as a mode of voluntary sacrifice, we can hardly say that this hierarchy is negative. Moreover, if hierarchy and heteronomy are understood through the lens of Christic embodiment, they are a hardly coercive means of control, but are invitational challenges that both Paul and the Corinthians reconfigure their relationships based on this image of Christ crucified.

8

Reading Paul Today

Convergence of Theology and Ethics

PAUL'S THEOLOGY AND ETHICS are informed by who God is, who Christ Jesus is, and who the believer (Paul) is. His thought and ethics are complex yet deeply spiritual and practical. Among the many aspects of Paul's theology and ethics is the idea that salvation or Christian identity is not secured once and for all because of Christ's vicarious death. It is the later epistles (Deutero-Pauline and Pastoral Letters) that understand Jesus' death in that way. These later epistles clearly present a two-step ethics based on "indicative to imperative mood." The indicative mode here refers to who you are. The imperative mode refers to what you should do. The deeper problem in this two-step ethics is that ethics can be separated from theology. Put differently, ethics (what you should do) cannot affect a person's identity (who you are) because one's salvation or identity is already established. That is, no matter what happens, an individual salvation or justification is secured once and for all.

However, as we saw in this book, Paul's theology involves the three aspects of God, Christ, and the believer in his historical ministry contexts. Furthermore, all of these aspects also involve the subjects' participation in a particular way: God's own righteousness, Christ's faithfulness, and the believer's life of Christ-like faith. Technically, it is impossible to separate theology from ethics or vice versa. The indicative force of one's identity cannot be separated from the imperative force of what one should do. A person's faithful life has both sides—indicative and imperative, theology and ethics, faith and action. In this regard, Paul's view of faith is not different from that of James: "a person is justified by works and not by faith alone; faith without works is also dead" (Jas 2:24, 26).[1] This saying of James may be evidence that there were some post-Pauline disciples who misunderstood Paul's gospel as the gospel of faith only. Jesus also tells a similar story about congruence between one's identity and work. A father says to the older brother: go and work in my vineyard. He said yes but never went to work. The younger son said no but went to work. The younger son is praised and worthy to be called son, not to say that he is not a son but because he is worthy of being identified as a son.[2]

Similarly, in the Hebrew Bible in general we can see this kind of congruency between a person's identity and ethics. "The one who is righteous shall live by faith" (Hab 2:4). "The blessed one is the one who does not sit with seat of the wicked" (Ps 1:2). There is no separation between a person's identity (status) and action (ethics). It is like saying that the indicative mood ("the one who is righteous") goes hand in hand with the imperative mood ("shall live by faith"). A person's indicative status (like "the one who is righteous") is not fixed or guaranteed apart from his or her action part ("shall live by faith"). We see a few examples in the Hebrew Bible: "Blessed is the one who meditates on the word of God" (Ps 1); "the righteous one shall live by faith" (Hab 2:4). The righteous one (theological identity) is the one who lives by faith (ethics). This verse was quoted in Rom 1:17 and Paul uses it in the same sense that theological identity is congruent with ethics. But Luther and his followers read Rom 1:17 to support the doctrine of justification by faith alone: "the righteous one by faith shall live."[3] Here "the righteous one by faith" (theological identity) means that one is justified by faith alone. But as we saw already, Paul's

---

1. In the Fourth Gospel as well, faith and action are not separated. Jesus, as the Son of God, the *logos*, comes to bring life and the light to the world. If people respond to the logos acting out of their faith, they stay in the light. So Jesus says: "If you continue in my word, you are truly my disciples" (John 8:31). Here Jesus addresses the Jews who believed in him and makes sure to communicate that belief needs to carry his word, implying that mere belief is not enough. Jesus' word here, among others, can point to his earlier talk to the disciples in 6:54: "Those who eat my flesh and drink my blood have eternal life." Participating in the way of Jesus (self-sacrificial love for others) is the way of living eternal life in the present, which will last forever.

2. Matt 21:28–32.

3. See Westerholm, *Perspectives Old and New on Paul*. In this book he examines the history of, and argues for, the doctrine of justification by faith.

view of faith involves complex relationships between God, Christ, and the believer. Even the believer's faith is to be informed by God and Christ. It also involves a lifelong commitment to God's love and Christ's faith. The danger of this two-step ethics (from the indicative to the imperative) is that the imperative force is treated as secondary to one's identity or theology. This does not make sense if we think of Paul's emphasis on an ongoing Christian journey and faith. As God's righteousness demands "a life worthy of God, who calls you into his own kingdom and glory" (1 Thess 2:12), Christians are to continue to participate in Christ's death (1 Cor 15:31; Gal 2:20).

As we see above, Paul's theology and ethics are inseparable, like the two sides of a coin. Paul's theology is ethics, and vice versa, because the three aspects of God, Christ, and the believer (God's righteousness, Christ's faithfulness, and the believer's living of Christ's body) contain theological, ethical imports. What this means is that in Paul's gospel, God is the only God from a Jewish theological perspective. Christ is the Son of God who embodies God's love and justice through his faithful obedience. Because of this faithfulness of Christ, God has dealt with all the former sins in the past (Rom 3:21–26) and ushered in a new time. But this new time and new creation is not granted to those who merely believe what Christ has done for them, but is experienced for those who participate in Christ's faith or death. This is where both theological and ethical aspects are manifest. Simply put, it is impossible to find a separation between the two.

A snapshot of the threefold theology of Paul is succinctly found in Rom 3:22: "The righteousness of God [God's righteousness] through the faith of Jesus Christ [Christ's faith] for all who believe [the believer's faith or participation in Christ]." Without the believer's participation in Christ, there will be no actual changes possible although God's righteousness is disclosed to the world through Christ's example. An analogy of the sun will be helpful. While the sun is available for all, if people do not come out into its light (believing that the sun is good and acting on that faith), their life will be still in darkness. In the Gospel of John's terms, Jesus as the incarnate Son of God brings life and light to the world, but the world does not accept him and hates him, fearing for their behavior to be disclosed. Even though God's love was embodied through Christ's life and death, the world is not welcoming of the message of love and justice. Even though Jesus is the way and the life in John's Gospel, the way of Jesus or the way of life cannot become the reality of everyday life if there is no living of the logos in their lives, carrying the message of love and justice, carrying the way of the cross and sacrifice for others. This idea of realism in the believer's life permeates Paul's letters. God justifies the one who has Christ's faith (Rom 3:26). The meaning of this verse is that God declares that he or she lives righteously through Christ-like faith. It is not about personal identity or a status of salvation once and for all; rather, it is about the believer's dynamic participation in Christ. As a result, his or her life is congruent with God's character of love and justice. In this context, this participation is what faith means. God "will justify the circumcised on the ground of faith and the uncircumcised through that same faith" (Rom 3:30).

All in all, Paul's thought and theology are hardly conceivable without the three-party involvement of God, Christ, and the believer. Paul's faith can be summarized as follows: "Die with Christ so that you may live for God"; and "You can live even though death-like situations engulf you." While the former emphasizes the sacrificial character of Jesus' life and the believer's participation in it, the latter stresses the believer's hope and victory against evil because of God's righteousness.

In closing, and in summary of this entire book, I list articles of Paul's faith below. This list is not in any way exhaustive but is indicative of his seamless theology expressed in his (authentic) letters. This list will be very helpful to those who study Paul for the first time, or for the first time again, because often Paul is a very complex, difficult, and even contradicting figure.

ARTICLES OF PAUL'S THEOLOGY:

- God is one, the God of both Jews and Gentiles.
- God loves all people—God's righteousness (*dikaiosyne theou*) is like the sun.
- God called and blessed Abraham to become the seed of all the whole human family.
- Abraham showed his trust (faith) in God's promise of this blessing.
- God continues to call people because they are marginalized.
- God gave the law to the Jews through Moses to guide and bless them.
- The centerpiece of the law is God's righteousness.

- God revealed Godself in creation and through people's hearts (conscience).
- Therefore Gentiles have no excuse.
- Both Jews and Gentiles failed to live according to God's righteousness because they did not act on the basis of faith. Jews had a zeal for the law, striving for their own righteousness but not acting on the basis of faith. Gentiles knew what was right but did not do it on the basis of faith (or conscience).
- As God is faithful, humans are expected to love God and their neighbors. But they failed because of their unwillingness to follow the principle of God's law (love and justice). The problem is not the law itself but the human heart problem.
- But Christ Jesus showed God's righteousness in the world through his life and death. Christ crucified is the true Messiah of God, declared to be the Son of God. Christ's faithfulness is his radical obedience to the love of God.
- Christ was crucified because of his challenge to the injustices of the world.
- Christ's death means a holy sacrifice for justice and solidarity with the marginalized people.
- Because of Christ's faith, God dealt with all former sins and declares a new time in Christ.
- Christ crucified is a new paradigm of life through which believers can participate in his faithfulness (*pistis christou*).
- The believer's participation in Christ's faithfulness means dying with Christ.
- As Jesus died, the believer should die to live (metaphorically). Death is enacted through baptism and remembered at the Lord's Supper. Dying with Christ means putting to death the deeds and practices of the flesh.
- The Spirit of God helps believers to fight the power of sin.
- The only way to win this fight is to put to death fleshly deeds through the help of the Sprit because sin exercises its power over the weak flesh.

- Fleshly desires or deeds mean the opposite of love—self-centered behaviors.
- God's children are those who live by the Spirit by putting to death the deeds of the flesh.
- Until the consummation, salvation is not complete.
- The language of election is heuristic, and everything is up to God's providence (mystery).

Bibliography

Agamben, Giorgio. *Homo Sacer: Sovereign Power and Bare Life*. Stanford, CA: Stanford University Press, 1995.
Althusser, Louis. "Ideology and Ideological State Apparatuses." In *Lenin and Philosophy, and Other Essays*. New York: Monthly Review Press, 1971.
Aristotle. *De Poetica* 1448b. Translated by I. Bywater. In *The Works of Aristotle*, edited W. D. Ross, vol. 11, Oxford: Clarendon, 1952.
Badiou, Alain. *Saint Paul: The Foundation of Universalism*. Stanford, CA: Stanford University Press, 2005.
Barcley, William B. *"Christ in You": A Study in Paul's Theology and Ethics*. Lanham, MD: University Press of America, 1999.
Barrett, C. K. *A Commentary on the First Epistle to the Corinthians*. New York: Harper & Row, 1968.
Bassler, Jouette. *Navigating Paul: An Introduction to Key Theological Concepts*. Louisville: Westminster John Knox, 2007.
Becker, Jürgen. *Paul: Apostle to the Gentiles*. Louisville: Westminster John Knox, 1993.
Beker, Christiaan. *Paul the Apostle: The Triumph of God in Life and Thought*. Philadelphia: Fortress, 1980.
Benjamin, Walter. "On the Mimetic Faculty." In *Reflections: Essays, Aphorisms, Autobiographical Writings*, edited by Peter Demetz, 333–36. New York: Harcourt Brace, 1987.
Berger, Peter, and Thomas Luckmann. *The Social Construction of Reality*. New York: Anchor, 1990.
Berger, Peter. *The Sacred Canopy: Elements of a Sociological Theory of Religion*. New York: Doubleday, 1967.
Borg, Marcus, and John Dominic Crossan. *The First Paul: Reclaiming the Radical Visionary behind the Church's Conservative Icon*. New York: HarperOne, 2009.
Boyarin, Daniel. *A Radical Jew: Paul and the Politics of Identity*. Berkeley: University of California Press, 1994.
Brown, Francis. *Hebrew English Dictionary*. Peabody, MA: Hendrickson, 1997.
Campbell, Douglas. *The Deliverance of God: An Apocalyptic Rereading of Justification in Paul*. Grand Rapids: Eerdmans, 2009.
Campbell, William. *Paul's Gospel in an Intercultural Context: Jew and Gentile in the Letter to the Romans*. Studies in the Intercultural History of Christianity 69. Frankfort: P. Lang, 1991.

Castelli, Elizabeth A. *Imitating Paul: A Discourse of Power*. Louisville: Westminster John Knox, 1991.

Coakely, Sarah. *Powers and Submissions: Spirituality, Philosophy and Gender*. Malden, MA: Blackwell, 2002.

Collins, John J. "Pre-Christian Jewish Messianism: An Overview." In *The Messiah in Early Judaism and Christianity*, edited by Magnus Zetterholm, 1–20. Minneapolis: Fortress, 2007.

Collins, Raymond. *First Corinthians*. Sacra pagina 7. Collegeville, MN: Liturgical, 1999.

Cosgrove, Charles. *Elusive Israel: The Puzzle of Election in Romans*. Louisville: Westminster John Knox, 1997.

Crossan, John Dominic. *The Birth of Christianity: Discovering What Happened in the Years Immediately after the Execution of Jesus*. San Francisco: HarperSanFrancisco, 1998.

Crossan, John Dominic, and Jonathan L. Reed. *In Search of Paul: How Jesus's Apostle Opposed Rome's Empire with God's Kingdom*. San Francisco: HarperSanFrancisco, 2004.

Danker, Fredrick W. *A Greek English Lexicon of the New Testament and Other Early Christian Literature*. 3rd ed. Chicago: University of Chicago Press, 2000.

Davidson, R. M. *Typology in Scripture: A Study of Hermeneutical Typos Structures*. Berrien Springs, MI: Andrews University, 1981.

De Boer, Willis Peter. *The Imitation of Paul: An Exegetical Study*. Kampen: Kok, 1960.

Dio Chrysostom. *Discourse*, 55.4–5. Edited by H. L. Crosby. Loeb Classics Library 4. London: Heinemann, 1946.

Donaldson, T. L. *Paul and the Gentiles: Remapping the Apostle's Convictional World*. Minneapolis: Fortress, 1997.

Donfried, Karl P. "The Cults of Thessalonica and the Thessalonian Correspondence." In *Paul, Thessalonica, and Early Christianity*, 21–48. Grand Rapids: Eerdmans, 2002.

Douglas, Mary. *Purity and Danger: An Analysis of the Concepts of Pollution and Taboo*. New York: Routledge, 1998.

Dunn, James D. G., editor. *Paul and the Mosaic Law*. Grand Rapids: Eerdmans, 2001.

———. *The Theology of Paul the Apostle*. Grand Rapids: Eerdmans, 1998.

Ehrensperger, Kathy. "Be Imitators of Me as I Am of Christ." *Lexington Theological Review* 38.4 (2003) 241–61.

———. *Paul and the Dynamics of Power: Communication and Interaction in the Early Christ-Movement*. Library of New Testament Studies 325. London: T. & T. Clark, 2009.

———. *That We May Be Mutually Encouraged: Feminism and the New Perspective in Pauline Studies*. London: T. & T. Clark, 2005.

Eisenbaum, Pamela Michelle. *Paul Was Not a Christian: The Real Message of a Misunderstood Apostle*. New York: HarperOne, 2009.

Ehrman, Bart D. *A Brief Introduction to the New Testament*. New York: Oxford University Press, 2007.

Elliott, Neil. *Liberating Paul: The Justice of God and the Politics of the Apostle*. Maryknoll, NY: Orbis, 1994.

———. *The Arrogance of Nations: Reading Romans in the Shadow of Empire*. Paul in Critical Contexts. Minneapolis: Fortress, 2008.

Elliott, Neil, and Mark Reasoner, editors. *Documents and Images for the Study of Paul*. Minneapolis, Fortress, 2010.

Fee, Gordon. *God's Empowering Presence: The Holy Spirit in the Letters of Paul*. Peabody, MA: Hendrickson, 2009.

Fiore, Benjamin. "Paul, Exemplification, and Imitation." In *Paul in the Greco-Roman World*, edited by J. Paul Sampley, 228–57. Harrisburg, PA: Trinity, 2003.

Fitzmyer, Joseph A. *First Corinthians: A New Translation with Introduction and Commentary*. Anchor Yale Bible 32. New Haven, CT: Yale University Press, 2008.
Furnish, Victor Paul. *The Theology of the First Letter to the Corinthians*. New Testament Theology. New York: Cambridge University Press, 1999.
Gaventa, Beverly Roberts. *Our Mother Saint Paul*. Louisville: Westminster John Knox, 2007.
Gillman, Neil. *The Death of Death: Resurrection and Immortality in Jewish Thought*. Woodstock, VT: Jewish Lights, 1997.
Grenholm, Cristina, and Daniel Patte. "Overture: Reception, Critical Interpretations, and Scriptural Criticism." In *Reading Israel in Romans: Legitimacy and Plausibility of Divergent Interpretations*, edited by Grenholm and Patte, 1–54. Romans through History and Cultures. Harrisburg, PA: Trinity, 2000.
———, editors. *Modern Readings of Romans*. Romans through History and Cultures. New York: T. & T. Clark, 2011 (forthcoming).
Grieb, A. Katherine. "So That in Him We Might Become the Righteousness of God" (2 Cor 5:21)." *Ex Auditu* 22 (2006) 58–80.
———. *The Story of Romans: A Narrative Defense of God's Righteousness*. Louisville: Westminster John Knox, 2002.
Jennings, Theodore W. *Transforming Atonement: A Political Theology of the Cross*. Minneapolis: Fortress, 2009.
Jervis, L. Ann. *At the Heart of the Gospel: Suffering in the Earliest Christian Message*. Grand Rapids: Eerdmans, 2007.
Jewett, Robert Jewett. *Romans: A Commentary*. Hermeneia. Minneapolis: Fortress, 2007.
Johnson, Luke Timothy. "Rom 3:21–26 and the Faith of Jesus." *CBQ* 44.1 (1982) 77–90.
Hamerton-Kelly, Robert G. "A Girardian Interpretation of Paul: Rivalry, Mimesis and Victimage in the Corinthian Correspondence." *Semeia* 33 (1985) 65–81.
Hampson, Daphne. "On Autonomy and Heteronomy." In *Swallowing a Fishbone?: Feminist Theologians Debate Christianity*, edited by Hampson, 1–16. London: SPCK, 1996.
Harrison, James R., *Paul and the Imperial Authorities at Thessalonica and Rome: A Study in the Conflict of Ideology*. Tübingen: Mohr, 2011 (forthcoming).
———. "Paul and the Imperial Gospel at Thessaloniki" *JSNT* 25.1 (2002) 71–96.
———. "The Imitation of the Great Man in Antiquity: Paul's Inversion of a Cultural Icon." In *Christian Origins and Classical Culture*, edited by Andrew Pitts. Leiden: Brill, 2010.
Hays, Richard B. "PISTIS and Pauline Christology: What Is at Stake?" In *Pauline Theology*, vol. 4: *Looking Back, Pressing On*, edited by E. Elizabeth Johnson and David M. Hay, 35–60. SBL Symposium Series 4. Atlanta: Scholars, 1997.
———. *The Faith of Jesus Christ: The Narrative Substructure of Galatians 3:1—4:11*. Biblical Resource Series. Grand Rapids: Eerdmans, 2002.
Horrell, David G. *The Social Ethos of the Corinthians Correspondence: Interest and Ideology from 1 Corinthians to 1 Clement*. Studies of the New Testament and Its World. Edinburgh: T. & T. Clark, 1996.
Horsley, Richard A. *1 Corinthians*. Abingdon New Testament Commentaries. Nashville: Abingdon, 1998.
———. *Paul and Empire: Religion and Power in Roman Imperial Society*. Valley Forge, PA: Trinity, 1997.
Hübner, Hans. *Law in Paul's Thought*. Edinburgh: T. & T. Clark, 1984.
Kahl, Brigitte. *Galatians Re-Imagined: Reading with the Eyes of the Vanquished*. Minneapolis: Fortress, 2010.
Käsemann, Ernst. *Commentary on Romans*. Translated and edited by Geoffrey W. Bromiley. Grand Rapids: Eerdmans, 1980.

———. "The Righteousness of God in Paul." In *New Testament Questions of Today*, 168–82. Philadelphia: Fortress, 1969.

———. "The Theological Problem Presented by the Motif of the Body of Christ." In *Perspectives on Paul*, translated by Margaret Kohl, 102–21. Philadelphia: Fortress, 1969.

Keck, Leander E. *Romans*. Abingdon New Testament Commentaries. Nashville: Abingdon, 2005.

Kelly, Michael, editor. "Mimesis." In *Encyclopedia of Aesthetics*, 3:233–46. New York: Oxford University Press, 1998.

Kim, Yung Suk. *Christ's Body in Corinth: The Politics of a Metaphor*. Paul in Critical Contexts. Minneapolis: Fortress, 2008.

———. "Imitators (*Mimetai*) in 1 Cor 4:16 and 11:1: A New Reading of Threefold Embodiment." *Horizons in Biblical Theology* 33.2 (2011, forthcoming).

Klawans, Jonathan. *Purity, Sacrifice, and the Temple: Symbolism and Supersessionism in the Study of Ancient Judaism*. New York: Oxford University Press, 2006.

Kooten, George H. *Paul's Anthropology in Context: The Image of God, Assimilation to God, and Tripartite Man in Ancient Judaism, Ancient Philosophy and Early Christianity*. WUNT 232. Tübingen: Mohr, 2008.

Laurance, John D. "The Eucharist as the Imitation of Christ." *Theological Studies* 47 (1986) 286–96.

Loewe, William P. *The College Student's Introduction to Christology*. Collegeville, MN: Liturgical, 1996.

Longenecker, Bruce W. *The Triumph of Abraham's God: The Transformation of Identity in Galatians*. Nashville: Abingdon, 1998.

Lopez, Davina C. *Apostle to the Conquered: Reimagining Paul's Mission*. Paul in Critical Contexts. Minneapolis: Fortress, 2008.

Mafico, Temba L. J. "Just, Justice." In *Anchor Bible Dictionary*, edited by David Noel Freedman, 3:1127–29. New York: Doubleday, 1992.

Malherbe, Abraham J. *The Letters to the Thessalonians: A New Translation with Introduction and Commentary*. Anchor Bible 32B. New York: Doubleday, 2000.

Marchal, Joseph A. *Hierarchy, Unity, and Imitation: A Feminist Rhetorical Analysis of Power Dynamics in Paul's Letter to the Philippians*. Atlanta: Society of Biblical Literature, 2006.

———. *The Politics of Heaven: Women, Gender, and Empire in the Study of Paul*. SBL Academia Biblica 24. Minneapolis, MN: Fortress Press, 2008.

Martin, Dale B. *Pedagogy of the Bible: An Analysis and Proposal*. Louisville: Westminster John Knox, 2008.

———. *The Corinthian Body*. New Haven, CT: Yale University Press, 1995.

McGrath, Alister E. *Iustitia Dei: A History of the Christian Doctrine of Justification*. New York: Cambridge University Press, 1986.

Mettinger, Tryggve N. D. *King and Messiah: The Civil and Sacral Legitimation of the Israelite Kings*. Lund: Gleerup, 1976.

Mitchell, Margaret. *Paul's Rhetoric of Reconciliation*. Louisville: Westminster John Knox, 1987.

Neyrey, Jerome. *Paul in Other Words: A Cultural Reading of His Letters*. Louisville: Westminster John Knox, 1990.

Oakes, Peter. "Re-Mapping the Universe: Paul and the Emperor in 1 Thessalonians and Philippians." *JSNT* 27.3 (2005) 301–22.

Odell-Scott, David W. *Paul's Critique of Theocracy: A/Theocracy in Corinthians and Galatians*. Journal for the Study of the New Testament: Supplement Series 250. London: T. & T. Clark, 2003.

Onesti, K. L., and M. T. Brauch. "Righteousness, Righteousness of God." In *Dictionary of Paul and His Letters*, edited by G. F. Hawthorne and R. P. Martin, 835. Downers Grove, IL: InterVarsity, 1993.
Owen, Paul. "The 'Works of the Law' in Romans and Galatians: A New Defense of the Subjective Genitive." *JBL* 126.3 (2007) 553–77.
Patte, Daniel. *The Gospel of Matthew: A Contextual Introduction for Group Study*. Nashville: Abingdon, 2003.
———. *Paul's Faith and the Power of the Gospel: A Structural Introduction to the Pauline Letters*. Philadelphia: Fortress, 1983.
———. *Preaching Paul*. Fortress Resources for Preaching. Philadelphia: Fortress, 1984.
Plato. *Timaeus* 38a–48e. Edited by J. Burnet and Platonis Opera. Oxford: Clarendon, 1905.
Polaski, Sandra Hack. *Paul and the Discourse of Power*. Gender, Culture, Theory 8. Sheffield: Sheffield Academic, 1999.
Price, James L. "God's Righteousness Shall Prevail." *Interpretation* 28.3 (1974) 259–80.
Räisänen, Heikki. *The Rise of Christian Beliefs: The Thought World of Early Christians*. Minneapolis: Fortress, 2010.
Reasoner, Mark. *Romans in Full Circle: A History of Interpretation*. Louisville: Westminster John Knox, 2005.
Roetzel, Calvin J. *Paul, a Jew on the Margins*. Louisville: Westminster John Knox, 2003.
———. *Paul: The Man and the Myth*. Studies on Personalities of the New Testament. Columbia: University of South Carolina Press, 1998.
———. *The Letters of Paul: Conversations in Context*. 5th ed. Louisville: John Knox Press, 2009.
Said, Edward W. *Humanism and Democratic Criticism*. Columbia Themes in Philosophy. New York: Columbia University Press, 2004.
Sanders, Boykin. "Imitating Paul: 1 Cor 4:16." *Harvard Theological Review* 74.4 (1981) 353–63.
Sanders, E. P. *Paul and Palestinian Judaism: A Comparison of Patterns of Religion*. Philadelphia: Fortress, 1977.
———. *Paul, the Law, and the Jewish People*. Philadelphia: Fortress, 1983.
Schüssler Fiorenza, Elisabeth. *The Power of the Word: Scripture and the Rhetoric of Empire*. Minneapolis: Fortress, 2007.
Scott, James C. *Domination and the Arts of Resistance: Hidden Transcripts*. New Haven, CT: Yale University Press, 1990.
Scullion, John J. "Righteousness (OT)." In *Anchor Bible Dictionary*, edited by David Noel Freedman, 5:724–36. New York: Doubleday, 1992.
Spariosu, Mihai, editor. *Mimesis in Contemporary Theory: An Interdisciplinary Approach*. 2 vols. Cultura Ludens 1. Philadelphia: J. Benjamins, 1984–91.
Stanley, D. M. "Become Imitators of Me" *Biblica* 40 (1959) 859–77.
Stendahl, Krister. *First Account: Paul's Letter to the Romans*. Minneapolis: Fortress, 1995.
———. *Paul among Jews and Gentiles, and Other Essays*. Philadelphia: Fortress, 1976.
———. "The Apostle Paul and the Introspective Conscience of the West." *Harvard Theological Review* 56.3 (1963) 199–215.
Steward, Roy A. *Rabbinic Theology*. London: Oliver and Boyd, 1961.
Stowers, Stanley Kent. *A Rereading of Romans: Justice, Jews, and Gentiles*. New Haven, CT: Yale University Press, 1994.
———. "Greeks Who Sacrifice and Who Do Not." In *The Social World of the First Christians: Essays in Honor of Wayne A. Meeks*, edited by L. Michael White and O. Larry Yabrough, 293–333. Minneapolis: Fortress, 1995.

Taussig, Michael. *Mimesis and Alterity: A Particular History of the Senses.* New York: Routeledge, 1993.
Theissen, Gerd. *The Social Setting of Pauline Christianity: Essays on Corinth.* Philadelphia: Fortress, 1982.
Thiselton, Anthony C. *First Corinthians: A Shorter Exegetical and Pastoral Commentary.* Grand Rapids: Eerdmans, 2006.
Virgil. *The Aeneid.* Translated by Robert Fagles. New York: Penguin, 2006.
Wallace, Daniel B. *Greek Grammar beyond the Basics: An Exegetical Syntax of the New Testament.* Grand Rapids: Zondervan, 1996.
Watson, Francis. *Paul, Judaism, and the Gentiles.* Grand Rapids, MI: Eerdmans, 2007.
Meeks, Wayne A. *The First Urban Christians: The Social World of the Apostle Paul.* 2nd ed. New Haven, CT: Yale University Press, 2003.
Welborn, L. L. *Paul, the Fool of Christ: A Study of 1 Corinthians 1–4 in the Cosmic-Philosophic Tradition.* Journal for the Study of the New Testament: Supplement Series 293. London: T. & T. Clark, 2005.
Westerholm, Stephen. *Perspectives Old and New on Paul: The "Lutheran" Paul and His Critics.* Grand Rapids: Eerdmans, 2004.
Wilhelm Michaelis. "Mimeomai." In *Theological Dictionary of the New Testament*, translated and edited by Geoffrey W. Bromiley, 4:666–73. Grand Rapids: Eerdmans, 1964–76.
Williams, Sam K. *Galatians.* Abingdon New Testament Commentaries. Nashville: Abingdon, 1997.
———. "The Righteousness of God in Romans." *JBL* 99.2 (1980) 242–90.
Wire, Antoinette C. *The Corinthian Women Prophets: A Reconstruction through Paul's Rhetoric.* Minneapolis: Fortress, 1990.
Wright, N. T. *What Saint Paul Really Said: Was Paul of Tarsus the Real Founder of Christianity?* Grand Rapids: Eerdmans, 1997.
———. *The Climax of the Covenant: Christ and the Law in Pauline Theology.* Minneapolis: Fortress, 1992.
Yeo, K. K., editor. *Navigating Romans through Cultures: Challenging Readings by Charting a New Course.* Vol. 3. Romans Through History and Cultures. London: T. & T. Clark, 2004.
Zetterholm, Magnus. *Approaches to Paul: A Student's Guide to Recent Scholarship.* Minneapolis: Fortress, 2009.
Žižek, Slavoj, Eric L. Santner, and Kenneth Reinhard. *The Neighbor: Three Inquiries in Political Theology.* Religion and Postmodernism. Chicago: University of Chicago Press, 2006.

Index

Abraham, 16, 40, 42, 49–50, 54, 59, 61, 64, 74, 78, 81, 86, 102, 134
Aeneas, 73
Aeneid, 45, 73
Agamben, Giorgio, 91
alternative community, 26
Althusser, Louis, 111n13
Amos, 41–42, 68
anthropology, 9, 114n22
Antioch, 35
Antiochus IV, 43n12
apocalyptic, 5, 7, 12–13, 25, 40, 43, 53, 55, 61, 69, 109n2
apostleship, 15n2, 34, 110
Arabia, 15n2
Aristotle, 113, 115
atonement, 3, 8, 60, 65, 79–80, 84
Augustine, 38, 65
autonomy, 117n34

Babylonian exile, 42, 43n12, 68
Badiou, Alain, 36n19
balance, 53, 67
Barcley, William, 34n17
Barrett, C.K., 110n5
Bassler, Jouette, 21n13, 24n2
Bathsheba, 87n6
Becker, Jürgen, 60n42
Beker, Christiaan, 12n16
Benjamin, Walter, 115
Berger, Peter, 10n11

blind pietism, 22
body: of Christ, 2–3, 6, 11, 18–19, 23–25, 28–30, 48n28, 52n33, 82–85, 92–93, 96–97, 100, 103–6, 108, 125, 127; Christ's, 3–4, 6, 13, 19, 24–25, 27–30, 33–34, 48n28, 52n33, 57, 76–77, 83, 85, 96–100, 103, 105–6, 112n15, 133; Christic, 3, 24, 83–85, 92, 103–4, 106–8, 123, 125, 127, 129; human, 10n10, 34, 97, 104–5; social, 9, 27, 28n9, 29, 52, 97–98, 100, 104–5, 123; spiritual, 52; sinful, 99–100, 123; one, 34, 105, 123, 127
Borg, Marcus, 14n20, 30n12, 45n17, 56n37, 122
bounded system, 9n9
Boyarin, Daniel, 110n8
burning bush, 87n7

Caesar Augustus, 45, 71, 73
Campbell, Douglas, 11n14, 25
Campbell, William, 20n9
Castelli, Elizabeth, 14n21, 110n4
Cephas, 35, 49, 123
chain of life (*see also* embodiment), 129
Christ crucified (*see also* cross *and* crucifixion), 11, 19, 24, 28n9, 29–30, 36n20, 52–53, 71–72, 76–77, 79, 85, 96, 100, 103, 108, 110, 112
Christ event, 11n14
Christian freedom, 74

143

Index

church (*ekklesia*): God's, 30, 48, 76, 85, 104; of Christ, 51n32; of God, 17, 26, 30, 35, 50, 51n32
Cicero, 113n21, 114
circumcision, 11, 17, 21, 35, 36, 50, 74n19, 86, 90, 94–95
Claudius, 32
Coakley, Sarah, 120n45
coexistence, 87
co-crucifixion, 36, 75
co-suffering, 75, 87, 95, 107
Collins, John, 68n10, 69n12, 70n14, 110n5
colonialism, 111–12
community organizer, 10, 109, 119
concord (*homonoia*), 9, 110
consummation, 12–13, 136
copy (*see also* sameness), 111–12, 114, 116, 118, 121–22, 128
Cosgrove, Charles, 54n35
covenantal nomism, 39n2
covenantal love, 16
crookedness, 74
cross (or crucifixion), 11, 13, 16–17, 22, 29–30, 33, 35–36, 50, 57, 60, 63, 66, 70–77, 80–82, 93, 95–96, 98, 102–3, 107, 116, 121–22, 126, 128, 134
Crossan, John Dominic, 4n10, 73n18, 122
Cyrus, 44, 67n7

Daniel, 43, 69–70
Davidson, R. M., 121n47
De Boer, Willis Peter, 112n14, 115, 121n47
deliberative rhetoric, 9n8, 110n4, 122
de(re)construction, 128
Dio Chrysostom, 113
discursive figurative structure, 125–26
Deutero-Pauline letters, 1n3, 15, 24n4, 29, 52n33, 56–58, 64, 79–80, 84–85, 95, 103–5, 120n44, 122, 129, 131
Deuteronomistic School, 42n11
diaspora, 4, 6, 38, 42, 45, 68, 71, 89, 108, 116, 119

dikaiosyne theou ("the righteousness of God"), 2–3, 5–6, 23, 25, 31, 38–40, 47, 53–54, 58, 60, 65–66, 80–81, 98, 133–34
disembodiment, 76, 125, 128
diversity, 7, 27–28, 34, 46, 50, 57, 68, 75, 91, 104, 109–11, 121, 125, 127, 129–30
Divi filius, 45
Donaldson, T. L., 16n4
Donfried, Karl, 47n22
Douglas, Mary, 9n9
dualism, 113
Dunn, James D. G., 11n14, 19n7, 21n13, 24n1, 38n1
dynamism, 97, 103, 105–6

ecclesiological, 28n9, 84, 104–5, 125
edification, 55
Ehrensperger, Kathy, 7n1, 30n12, 112n14, 116n33, 122n49
Ehrman, Bart, 56n37
Eisenbaum, Pamela, 39n5
Eli, 88n9
Elkanah, 88n9
Elliott, Neil, 14n20, 45n17, 62n43, 71n16, 92n12, 114n26
embodiment, 29, 53, 57, 66, 76, 81, 83–84, 106, 109, 112, 116–17, 120–23, 125–30
Emunah, 64
Enoch, 69
enlightened passion, 4
Essenes, 44n15
eternal life, 43n14, 56–57, 132
ethics, x, 6, 9, 41, 55, 93, 96, 129, 131–33
evil, 12, 25, 33, 37, 40, 44n15, 55, 57, 61, 66, 74, 77, 80–81, 84, 93, 95, 101, 134
exclusivism, 8, 32
Ezra and Nehemiah, 68

faith: in Christ, 1, 3, 7–8, 10, 12, 21, 24, 28n9, 33, 39, 65, 79–80, 99, 120n44; in God, 27, 47–50, 58, 66, 71, 73–74, 93, 101, 134; of Christ,

2–3, 6, 18, 20n12, 21, 23–25, 31, 65, 80, 92, 102; Christ's, ix, x, 3–4, 6, 8, 10, 12–13, 16–17, 21, 23–25, 28, 31–33, 35–37, 39, 57–58, 60–63, 65–66, 71–83, 92, 95, 98, 101–2, 108, 120–21, 128–29, 131, 133–35; object of, 3, 65, 79; Christ-like, 11, 93, 131, 134; the law of, 21, 102; and the law, 21, 36; Christ's life of, 75, 77; and works, 80; Abraham's, 78; the subject of, 79; Paul's, 102, 120n44, 126, 134

Faithfulness, 10, 16, 18, 23, 31, 33, 39–42, 49, 54, 59–60, 62, 66, 70–71, 73, 79, 82, 85, 95, 108, 114, 117, 120–22, 128–29, 131, 135

fate, 114
Fee, Gordon, 1n1, 110n5
Fides, 64, 114
final judgment, 12, 52
Fiore, Benjamin, 14n21, 110n5
Fitzmyer, Joseph, 110n5
forensic salvation, 5, 7–9, 14, 109n2
Fourth Philosophy, 44n15
functionalist sociology, 9
Furnish, Victor, 110n5

Gaventa, Beverly, 12n17, 13n18
gender inequality, 14
genitive: subjective, 2–4, 12, 19, 21, 23–25, 31, 39–40, 47, 54, 60, 63n1, 65–66, 72, 78, 80, 100, 120n44, 129; objective, 2–4, 7, 12–13, 21, 24–25, 28, 38, 47n26, 78, 80, 123; attributive, 2–3, 21, 23–25, 85, 92, 99, 123, 125
Gentile Christians, 32, 35–36, 46, 48–49, 53–54, 56, 61, 77n23, 100
Gillman, Neil, 43n12
Girardian interpretation, 119
God's house or household, 20n10, 66, 94
good news: *see* Gospel
Gospel: of God, 1, 16, 31–33, 47–49, 54, 58, 61, 72, 77–78, 92, 94, 101; of Christ, 35, 47n26, 48–49, 72–74, 78, 94, 101–2; Paul's, ix, x, 6, 8, 13–14,

20n9, 25–26, 32–33, 35, 38, 49, 51, 57, 62–63, 75, 95, 101, 132–33; God's, ix, 13, 32, 47–49, 54, 57–59, 61–62, 72, 75–77, 81–83, 95; imperial, 47; different, 35–36, 48–49, 74n19; the concept of, 57
Greco-Roman world, 6, 38, 63, 122
Grieb, A. Katherine, 31n14

Halaka, 83n1
Hamerton-Kelly, Robert, 119
Hampson, Daphne, 120n45
Hannah, 88n9
Harrison, James, 47, 114n24
Hays, Richard, 58n38, 65n3
Hellenism, 89
Hellenistic philosophy, 52
Herod the Great, 45n20, 90
Hesed, 41, 81
heteronomy, 107, 117–20, 130
hidden transcripts, 118
hierarchical unity, 27, 45–46, 90, 104, 113–14, 129
hilasterion (or mercy seat), 60, 80
history and theology, 4–5, 42n10
holiness, 31, 40, 48, 54, 66–68, 81
holism, 97, 103, 105–6
Holy Spirit, 1, 15n2, 55, 84, 105, 107
Homo sacer, 91, 101
honor and shame, 34
Horrell, David, 119n41
Horsley, Richard, 14n20, 47n22, 57n31
Hosea, 68, 87
household code, 30n11
Hübner, Hans, 24n1, 50n29
human: agency, 13; disobedience, 9; endorsement, 15n2; flesh, 13, 33; heart, 60, 90, 108, 135; participation, ix, 12, 23, 83, 92; problems, 2, 85, 94

idealistic missionary, 15n2
identity, 9–10, 28, 30, 49, 57, 65, 68, 90, 128, 131–34
ideology, 13, 16, 30, 34, 45, 52, 61, 91, 111n12, 113–15

idolatry, 12–13, 25
idols, 28, 48, 51, 124n58, 128
imagination, 5, 108
imitation. *See mimesis*
imperative, 131–33
impurity, 9n9, 89
in Christ, 1, 3–4, 7–10, 12–13, 16–19, 21–22, 24–26, 28–29, 33–34, 36, 39, 50–51, 53, 56–57, 60, 62, 65–66, 72, 74–76, 79–80, 82–84, 95, 98–103, 106, 116, 120–22, 124–29, 133–35
indicative, 131–34
institution, 29–30, 106
interpolation, 30

Jennings, Theodore, 8nn4–6, 9n7
Jeremiah, 68, 88, 90, 94
Jerusalem church, 15n2, 48
Jervis, L. Ann, 12n17
Jesus movement, 63n1
Jewett, Robert, 19n8
Jewish: Christianity, 35; customs, 35, 74n19; ethnocentrism, 11, 32, 49, 74n19; Pseudepigrapha, 69; tradition, ix, 22, 45, 48, 71, 81, 95, 108; roots, 4
Jews and Gentiles, 1, 11, 20n10, 22, 32, 37, 39, 45, 49, 54, 59, 61, 63, 66, 72, 94, 134–35
Jonah, 88, 94
Judaism, 4–6, 11–12, 14–18, 20, 32, 36, 38–39, 42, 54, 68–69, 89–90
Jupiter, 46, 54, 73
justice: retributive, 39; distributive, 39–40, 42, 52–53, 93
justification: imputed or imparted, 38; individual, x, 5, 9n11, 39, 41, 84, 92; by faith, 5, 132

Kahl, Brigitte, 45n17
Käsemann, Ernst, 31n14, 58n38, 85n2
karath, 86
Keck, Leander, 29n10, 31n13, 60n41
Kelly, Michael, 112n16
kenosis, 120n45

Kim, Yung Suk, 3n8, 24n3, 28n8, 48n28, 95n14, 112n15, 114n23, 120n42, 123n52, 124nn57–58
kingship, 67
King David, 67
Klawans, Jonathan, 86n3
kyros, 45

Lament Psalm, 87n6
Laurance, John, 121n46
Law/law: of Christ, 50, 75, 95; dying to the, 18–19, 21–22, 35, 100, 103; the emperor's, 31; the end of the, 18, 20; the essence of the, 50; the goal of the, 20, 32; of God, 9, 13, 16, 18–19, 21, 33, 37, 100; God's, 2, 18–19, 21–22, 24, 32–33, 100, 135; misuse of the, 21; Mosaic, 18, 60n40; of sin, 18–19, 100; of the Spirit, 18, 22; without faith, 36, 50, 103; zeal for the, 22, 34, 50n29, 61, 74n19, 102, 135
leadership, 30, 70
legalism, 11n14, 20, 39n2, 59
life and peace, 13, 19, 22, 31–32
Livy, 27n7, 114n23
Loewe, William, 8n4
Logos, 132n1, 134
Longenecker, Bruce, 12n16
Lopez, Davina, 17n6, 45n17, 73n17
Lord's Supper, 28, 51, 96–97, 124n58, 127–28, 135
love and justice, 2n4, 17, 22, 32n16, 47–51, 55, 58–59, 61–62, 66, 68, 73–76, 81–82, 87, 94–96, 99, 101, 106, 108, 117, 122, 133–35
love patriarchalism, 10n10, 119
Luther, 38, 65, 132

Maccabees, 44
Mafico, Temba, 41n8
Malherbe, Abraham, 46n21, 47n25
Marchal, Joseph, 14n21, 110n4, 111n10
Martin, Dale, 110, 111n12
Meeks, Wayne, 119n41
Menenius, 27, 114

McGrath, Alister, 38
Messiah, 69–71
Messianic kingdom, 44
metaphor, 3, 9–11, 17, 24, 27, 29–30, 34, 75, 83–86, 93, 95–98, 100, 103–6, 108, 125
Mettinger, Tryggve, 67n6
Micah, 42
Michaelis, Wilhelm, 110n4
mimesis (imitation), 110, 112–13, 115–16, 118
mimetai (imitators), x, 109–13, 123
mimetic faculty, 115
mimicry, 110n4, 111, 115, 118
Mispat, 41, 81
Mitchell, Margaret, 9n8, 10n13, 110nn4–5
moral development, 116
moral sacrifice (*see also* sacrifice), 8, 96
Moses, 50n29, 87n7, 89, 134
mutual crucifixion, 17, 36, 75

narcissism, 4n10
neighbor, 4n9, 23, 41, 51, 55, 61, 88, 95, 101, 135
new creation, 17, 22, 36, 53–55, 95, 98, 133
new hope, 82
new life, 17, 22, 25, 33, 42
New Perspective on Paul, 5, 7, 11, 21n13, 39n2, 66, 109
Nineveh, 88

Oakes, Peter, 47n23
obedience, 3, 9, 16, 18, 31–32, 37, 42, 46, 59–60, 63, 66, 73–74, 77–78, 80, 117, 120, 122, 133, 135
Odell-Scott, David, 123
old self, 19, 99
Onesimus, 56, 78, 103
organism, 3, 10–11, 24n4, 27–30, 34, 84–85, 97, 104
Owen, Paul, 20n11

Palestine, 11, 44, 69

paradigm shift, 71
participation, ix, 2–4, 6, 8–9, 12–13, 23–25, 28, 30, 38, 58, 63, 66, 76, 79–80, 83, 92, 95, 106, 114n21, 120–21, 126–29, 131, 133–35
patron-client system, 34, 115, 120
Patte, Daniel, 111n12
Pastoral letters, ix, 1n2, 15, 56–58, 64, 79–80, 104, 122, 131
Paul's letters, ix-x, 1–2, 6, 13, 25, 30, 38, 46, 48, 63, 72, 79–80, 83–85, 92, 99, 103–4, 109n2, 110, 120, 129, 134
Pauline interpretation, 4–5, 7, 109n2
peace, 2, 13, 16, 19, 21–22, 24, 31–33, 36, 45–47, 52, 55–57, 61–62, 67–68, 78, 85, 93–95, 98, 101, 114, 119
peacemaking, 57
penal substitution, 8, 21n12, 65, 79, 84
persecutor, 15–16, 102
Persian Empire, 42
Pharisees, 44n15, 76, 90
Philemon, 1n3, 56, 78, 101, 103
pistis christou (*see also* "faith of Christ"), 2–3, 23, 25, 58n38, 60, 62, 63, 65–66, 74, 76, 79–80, 129, 135
Plato, 112–13, 115
Polaski, Sandra, 14n21, 110n4, 111n9
political theology, 4n9
positivism, 4n10
post-colonial, 111, 118
power structure, 14, 26, 67
Price, James, 40n6
promise, 16, 22, 31, 40, 49–51, 54, 58–59, 61, 74, 134
Psalms of Solomon, 69
public scripts, 118
purity, 9n9, 10, 68, 86n3, 89, 109n2

Qoom, 86
Qumran, 44, 70

Rabbinic theology, 43n13
Räisänen, Heikki, 42n10, 44n16
ransom theory, 8, 65n4

Reasoner, Mark, 8n3, 20n11, 45n17, 65n3
reductionism, 8
relationality, 117n34
resistance, 44, 90
resurrection, 11n14, 29, 31, 43, 51–52, 54, 71, 81–82, 96, 106
Revelation, 15n2, 43, 71, 107, 127
reward, 40, 43, 55
righteousness: from God, 1, 3, 7–8, 18, 23, 38; of God, 2–3, 5–6, 23, 25, 31, 38–40, 47, 54, 58, 60, 80, 98, 133; God's, x, 2–4, 8–10, 13, 16, 19–25, 27, 31, 33, 35–51, 53–56, 58–62; human, 11, 24; individual, 1, 3, 7–8, 21, 38–39, 65; our own, 3
Roetzel, Calvin, 16n3, 47n27, 74n20
role: of the believer, 3, 10, 12, 65, 79, 92; of Christ, 3, 13, 39, 47n26, 60, 63, 66, 75, 78–79, 124n57; of God, 8, 10, 12–13, 15, 49, 51, 54, 56
Roman Empire (see also Rome), ix, 4, 16, 29, 31, 40, 43, 45–46, 51, 55, 62, 66, 71, 73, 84, 89–91, 93, 101, 111, 113–14, 119, 122, 130
Rome, 31–33, 45, 53–54, 61–62, 70, 73, 77

sacrifice, x, 3, 8–9, 13, 16–17, 21n12, 27, 29–30, 32n16, 35, 39, 52, 56–57, 60, 65, 67–68, 71, 75, 77–81, 84, 86–87, 89–91, 93, 96–97, 100–102, 104, 108, 120–21, 124–25, 128–30, 134–35
Sadducees, 44n15
Said, Edward, 4n10
salvation, 2, 5, 7–9, 11–14, 20, 23–24, 28, 31, 33, 36–37, 39, 44, 54, 56–61, 65, 70, 72, 74, 79, 92, 100, 102, 109n2, 131, 134, 136
sameness (see also copy), 111–12, 115
Sanders, E. P., 11, 21n13, 39n2
Sanders, Boykin, 30n12, 112n14, 122n49
satisfaction theory, 8, 21n12, 65, 84
scapegoat, 89, 119
Schüssler Fiorenza, Elisabeth, 14n21

Scott, James, 114n25, 118n35
Scullion, John, 40n7
Second Temple Judaism, 4, 6, 38, 42n10, 68–69, 90
self-criticism, 9
self-seeking glory, 17, 45, 51, 76–77, 128
Seneca, 114n21
sin (see also evil), 2, 4n10, 11n14, 12–13, 18–20, 22–25, 32–33, 35–37, 39–40, 77, 87, 92, 98–100, 122–23, 135
social: accommodation, 30; being, 9; body (see also organism), 9, 27, 28n9, 29, 52, 97–98, 100, 104–5, 123; canopy, 10
social-scientific/sociological, 5, 7, 9–10, 109n2, 118–19
sociology of knowledge, 10
solidarity, 11, 19, 22, 24, 30, 35, 37, 76, 80, 87n7, 90, 93, 95–96, 98, 106, 135
soma christou. See the "body of Christ"
somatic, 84–85
Son of God, 21, 46, 47n26, 54, 80–81, 104, 113, 121–22, 132n1, 133, 135
Son of Man, 69–70
Spanish mission, 54
Spariosu, Mihai, 118n37
spiritual elitism, 76n22
spirituality, 87, 108
Stendahl, Krister, 11n14, 17n5, 39
Stoicism/Stoics, 45, 46, 97, 115, 117, 120, 122, 124–25
Stowers, Stanley, 60n41, 64n2, 90
Suetonius, 32
suffering, 12, 40, 43, 55, 61, 75–77, 87–92, 95–96, 99, 102, 105, 107–8, 112
super-apostles, 51, 76
symbolic: boundary, 9n9; universe, 10–11

Taussig, Michael, 118
telos nomou, 20
Theissen, Gerd, 10n10, 119
theocentric, 13, 51n32
theodicy, 12, 40, 43
Thiselton, Anthony, 110n5

threefold: approach, 4; aspects, xi, 25; formula, 1, 26, 31, 34; language, 129; relationship, 121; theology, 2, 4–6, 15, 23, 25–26, 31–32, 36–38, 63, 83, 100, 107, 133

Timaeus, 112n16, 113n18

transformation, 75, 82, 101, 106–8

uncircumcision, 17, 36, 50, 95
unfaithfulness, 1, 16, 18, 23, 33
unity, 9, 14, 27–29, 34, 45–46, 57, 75, 90, 97, 103–5, 110, 113, 117, 122, 124–26, 129
universalism, 111
Uriah, 87n6

vicarious death, 65, 131
Virgil, 45, 73

Welborn, Laurence, 26n6, 110n4, 122–23, 124n56
Watson, Francis, 10n12
way of life, 10n12, 24, 29–30, 32–33, 35, 47, 53, 61, 95, 97–98, 100, 103, 105–6, 112, 116–17, 120, 122, 124–25, 128, 133

Westerholm, Stephen, 132n3
Williams, Sam, 31n14, 58n38
Wire, Antoinette, 14n21
wisdom, 11, 22, 24, 26, 28, 32, 35, 51–52, 56, 61, 77, 96, 112n15, 124, 126, 128
works of the law (or *erga nomou*), 11, 18, 20–21, 35
works righteousness, 11, 20, 39n2, 59
wrath, 39–40, 72, 74
Wright, N. T., 11n14, 12n15, 21n13, 39n4

zeal, 19, 21–22, 32n16, 34, 48, 50n29, 54, 61, 74n19, 99, 102, 135
Zechariah, 68
Zerubbabel, 69
Zetterholm, Magnus, 7n2
Zeus, 54
Žižek, Slavoj, 4n9

www.ingramcontent.com/pod-product-compliance
Lightning Source LLC
Chambersburg PA
CBHW022122160426
43197CB00009B/1123